Chase That Itch

The Power of Embracing Failure
to Fall Forward to Achieve your Goals

AUAHATIA

First published by Ultimate World Publishing 2024
Copyright © 2024 AUAHATIA

ISBN

Paperback: 978-1-923123-90-8
Ebook: 978-1-923123-91-5

AUAHATIA has asserted her rights under the Copyright, Designs and Patents Act 1988 to be identified as the author of this work. The information in this book is based on the author's experiences and opinions. The publisher specifically disclaims responsibility for any adverse consequences which may result from use of the information contained herein. Permission to use information has been sought by the author. Any breaches will be rectified in further editions of the book.

All rights reserved. No part of this publication may be reproduced, stored in or introduced into a retrieval system, or transmitted in any form, or by any means (electronic, mechanical, photocopying, recording or otherwise) without the prior written permission of the author. Any person who does any unauthorised act in relation to this publication may be liable to criminal prosecution and civil claims for damages. Enquiries should be made through the publisher.

Cover design: Ultimate World Publishing
Layout and typesetting: Ultimate World Publishing
Editor: Vanessa McKay

Ultimate World Publishing
Diamond Creek,
Victoria Australia 3089
www.writeabook.com.au

Testimonials

Having walked alongside Hazel for much of her career I was really excited when Hazel said she was going to write a book. From her early 20's, Hazel was such a go-getter. She was always keen to learn, she always had a next goal and she always aspired to be the best. Every goal she set she achieved from sports coordinator to leading a course at Polytech, becoming a Principal, to getting her PhD, to lecturing at University, a senior lecturer and now becoming a Te Kaiwhakatere - Director of Māori Development. One of the things I have always admired about Hazel is her strong sense of justice. She is not afraid to speak up when things are morally wrong. She sets high standards for herself and believes we should all aspire to high standards.

One of Hazel's dreams is to see better education for Māori at all levels of the system. She has a passion for academia and would like to see more Māori entering University and succeeding. In her book Chase That Itch, Hazel shares her journey through education and her trials and tribulations. The learnings she had and the uncanny knack she developed for falling forward when many would have taken steps backward, have fueled her to write a compelling story that inspires others and lights the way to assist the reader in their journey.

Hazel has many dreams and passion for them all. Coaching and mentoring, young Māori to navigate the education system, attend and succeed at University, and go on to be part of research and academia is a vision she sees on the horizon. Chase That Itch will inspire many young achievers and if they are lucky enough to get the opportunity to work with Hazel they will find rich rewards.

Along with writing, Hazel plans to speak her truth. As a guest speaker, I see she will shine her light and continue growing with her vision and chasing the next itch. This is part of who she is. Hazel's first book shares much of herself in a way that allows the reader to really relate. I hope you enjoy knowing Hazel as much as I do.

Jenny Tebbutt

Disclaimer

The content of this book is based on the author's personal experiences and perspectives. The tips and wisdom shared are intended to provide guidance and insight into chasing dreams and working through challenging situations and dilemmas. Readers are encouraged to use their judgment and discretion when applying the information to their lives. The sharing of stories is meant to foster connection and understanding, but readers should interpret them in the context of the author's individual experiences. The author advises readers to seek professional guidance where necessary if sensitive material may trigger and unravel loss and grief associated with a traumagenic event in their life.

Waikato Whānau

Uncle George

Dedication

This heartfelt message expresses deep gratitude and appreciation for the love and support from family and friends. As I have broken through glass ceilings in my education, workplace, and personal life. My sentiments broken down include:

Gratitude to Dad: I am grateful to my dad for being a positive role model and for providing a lifetime full of guidance and wisdom. My dad has always been my number one supporter and has instilled a deep faith of learning, encouraged me to pursue my dreams, stand steadfast and run head-on into a storm.

Inspiration of Mum: My mum is an inspirational woman who, over her lifetime, has continuously overcome adversity. Her resiliency and determination are a gift that has been given to me.

Family and Friends: The journey from my humble beginnings to achieving professional success is attributed to the unwavering support of family and friends. Who would have thought that this country girl from Wairoa and Te Teko would become an emerging Māori researcher specializing in *mātauranga Māori* (Māori knowledge) and lecturing at Auckland University of Technology (AUT) in New Zealand.

Gratitude to my siblings, their partners and my nieces, grandniece, and nephews: I am grateful for all of your support in a dark and turbulent chapter of my life. I will be indebted to you for eternity.

Gratitude to Sherlock Bones: The most loyal friend a girl could ever have in life. Sherlock brought joy and peace and provided me with unconditional love as my only *whangai* (adoptee) fur baby.

Encouragement to others: This message concludes with a wish for others facing difficult times and looking for comfort. I encourage you to reach out to someone for support. Breathe slowly and deeply and know I offer these words of solace and empowerment shared with me in my time of despair:

"You will get through it."

Foreword

Welcome to this book, where the journey of chasing your dreams and navigating through life's challenges are explored. The essence of having a vision is emphasised, as it brings clarity and purpose to your life, guiding you toward your dreams. Dealing with complex situations and dilemmas can take you off track from your dreams and purpose in life. Without a clear purpose, life may lose its meaning, but with a defined vision, life becomes vibrant and purposeful.

The importance of having a plan is underscored, as it is crucial to success. By neglecting to plan, you are planning to fail, missing opportunities for personal growth and self-realisation. The content of this book is structured around real-life events experienced by the author, providing a chronological narrative that offers valuable insights and wisdom.

In addition to practical tips, this book offers a unique feature – the opportunity to "share a story" about the author's experiences in chasing her dreams. This storytelling aspect encourages reflection and the development of a growth mindset and a positive attitude, essential for overcoming challenges and evolving into a better version of oneself.

Embracing a go-getter attitude and understanding how challenges can foster personal growth and real-lived leadership are key themes explored in this book.

May this book inspire you to pursue your dreams with determination and resilience, and may the stories shared within serve as a source of motivation and guidance on your journey towards personal fulfilment and success.

Dr Haze

Contents

Foreword	9
Introduction	13
1. Nurturing the leader from the beginning	21
2. The importance of education and educational experiences in cultivating leadership skills	37
3. Inspiring dreams through familial support and encouragement from educators	45
4. The university years of experimentation and living my purpose	65
5. Transitioning from university to the workplace	91
6. Transitioning from Te Kauwhata to Auckland	109
7. Courage to grow and invest time on personal relationships and career advancement	117
8. Daring to be brave to chase a PhD and home ownership	135
9. The Storm Before the Calm	147
10. Getting back on track	163
11. Strengthening connections to *te ao Māori* (Māori world)	181
12. The power of new adventures	187
13. Guide points for life	199
Afterword	209
About The Author	211
Glossary	213
References	217
Appendix 1: The story of Te Teko	221

> *Authentic leadership stems from the lived experiences that shape our character, reminding us that every challenge we face is a stepping stone toward becoming a resilient leader.*

Introduction

Growing into an authentic leader through lived experiences

Thank you for committing to supporting me. You are turning up and are showing your open to learning and listening without trying to fix or win. As you begin to read, I share and introduce the learnings from my personal memories which capture the essence of authentic leadership and its foundation in my lived experiences. Embark on a transformative journey with me as I delve deep into the extraordinary realms of personal and professional growth. Through the lens of my own lived experiences, I aim to uncover the profound intersections that shape our paths and mould our futures. Courageously stepping forward, I will share how I navigated the unknown with bravery and resilience, over geographical time, and space. This narrative is a testament to the unwavering human spirit, how to dare to dream big and turn obstacles into stepping stones for success. My story serves as a beacon of hope, challenging us to reframe our perspectives on setbacks and losses. By embracing the notion that failure adds value to our journey, we can push past our limitations and pursue our deepest desires.

I start with the seeding of my dream and the importance of being nurtured as a child by my first teachers – my parents and family.

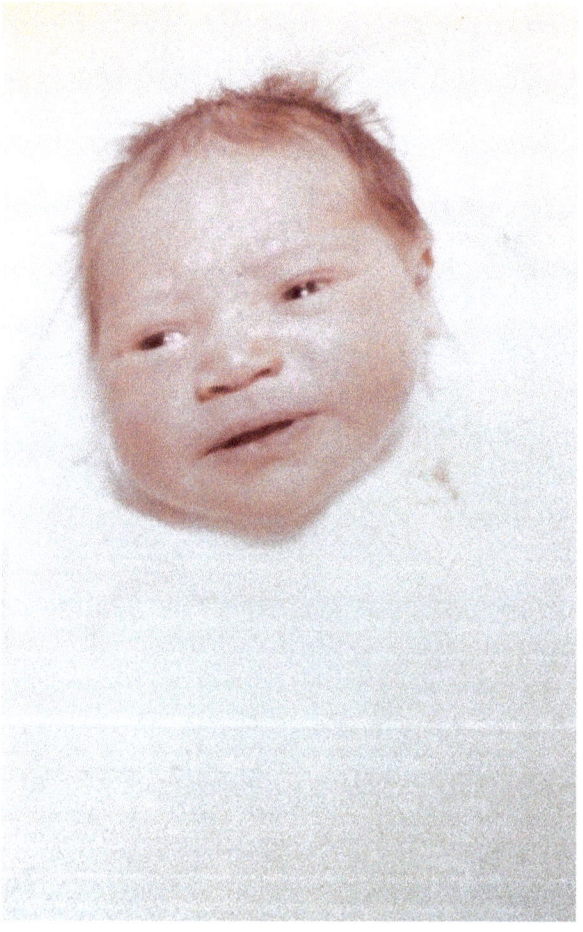

Hazel's entry into the world on the 21 September 1977

Introduction

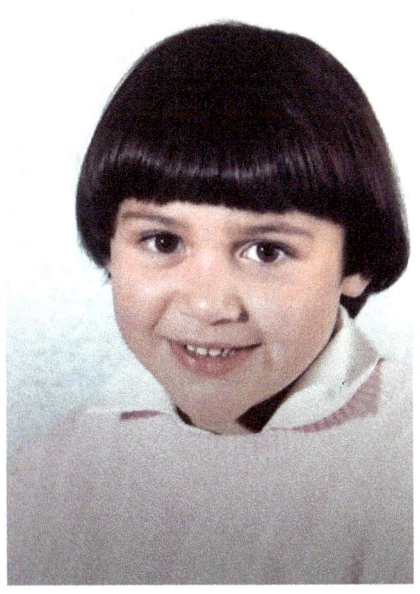

**Hazel at five years old
Her first school was Pink Carroll Primary in Wainuiomata**

The seeding of the dream and nurturing of the child

Since my childhood, I have always believed that exceptional fathers like my dad exemplify integrity and lead with honour. My dad demonstrated to me the importance of leading a family with integrity, as well as how to raise, nurture, and guide children to reach their full potential, embodying the qualities of *mana* (prestige, authority, control, power, influence, status, spiritual strength, and charisma). My mother not only taught me the importance of resilience but also demonstrated how to embody *tinorangatiratanga* (self-determination) in challenging circumstances. Both my mother's and father's wisdom have influenced my genetic makeup. The environment I am surrounded by and the individuals I choose to have in my life have also played a significant role in shaping my core beliefs. It is through the guidance of my parents and living life that has moulded me into the person I am today.

My parents bestowed me the name Hazel as a tribute to my grandmother and my Māori name, 'Aroha.' Aroha perfectly encapsulates my natural traits of love, empathy, and positivity. This name holds a special place in my heart, reminding me of the importance of selflessness and kindness in influencing and serving the people I am close to in my life.

In the enthralling journey of life, the pursuit of dreams serves as the driving force that propels people like me toward self-discovery, resilience, and eventual triumph. This book embarks on a captivating exploration of a riveting odyssey, of taking a deep dive into the many myriad of lessons learned while navigating life and chasing one's dreams. As the author, my primary aim is to highlight the path for others aiming to take on the challenge of embarking on a university education in New Zealand and gaining an in-depth insight into overcoming setbacks of a personal and professional nature.

From the formative years of my childhood to the challenges faced as a Māori student navigating the intricate landscape of mainstream education in New Zealand, leaving home as a fourteen-year-old, and embarking on a university education as a first in family, the narrative weaves through the tapestry of personal growth and development. The spotlight then shifts to the professional realm, where twenty-three years of lived experiences across the primary, secondary, and tertiary education sectors in New Zealand become the crucible for developing insights and wisdom.

This book focuses on authenticity and the perspective of an insider researcher (a researcher from the communities she comes from Ngāti Awa and Ngāti Tūwharetoa), blending personal and professional aspects

Introduction

to give readers a close look into the life of a Māori woman striving to achieve her dreams. The stories shared capture the challenges faced, the strength required, and the successes attained, both in the author's career and personal life. By presenting the journey through both a Māori and Pākehā viewpoint, readers gain a special and authentic insight into the struggles of a Māori woman pursuing her aspirations and the transformative journey of becoming a lived experienced leader within the Western Academy.

The obstacles and trials we encounter in life are what mould our identity and give us the chance to grow into stronger leaders. Let this book motivate and embolden you to welcome the unfamiliar, taking courageous strides towards discovering your authentic self. Together, we can light the way for all who are brave enough to follow their dreams.

From my perspective, authentic leadership is a leadership style that emphasises transparency, genuineness, and honesty. Let me break down the key elements you will come across:

1. ***Authentic Leadership:*** The concept of authentic leadership emphasises genuineness, transparency, and a deep connection to be with one's true self. Authentic leaders are not afraid to show vulnerability and are committed to being true to their values.

2. ***Lived Experiences influence character:*** The acknowledgment that lived experiences shape our character suggests that the authenticity of a leader is deeply rooted in personal growth and development. Each experience contributes to the uniqueness of an individual's character.

3. ***Challenges are stepping stones:*** Viewing challenges as stepping stones implies a positive and growth-oriented mindset. Authentic leaders recognize that overcoming obstacles is an integral part of their journey, leading to personal and professional development.

4. ***Resilience as a leadership trait:*** The statement links challenges to resilience, highlighting that facing difficulties head-on contributes to the development of resilience. Resilience is a crucial quality for effective leadership, enabling individuals to navigate uncertainties and setbacks.

5. ***A continuous journey of becoming:*** The phrase "stepping stone toward becoming" implies that authentic leadership is a continuous process of growth. It suggests that leaders are not static; instead, they are continually evolving through their experiences.

6. ***Reminder of the transformative power:*** The statement serves as a reminder that challenges, rather than being roadblocks, have the potential to transform individuals. Each challenge becomes an opportunity for learning and becoming a stronger, more resilient leader.

In summary, authentic leadership is deeply intertwined with personal experiences, especially the challenges faced. Come with me on a journey of self-exploration and personal development, where endless opportunities are waiting for those who have the courage to pursue their aspirations. The journey of facing and overcoming challenges not only shapes an individual's character but also contributes to the development of resilience, a key attribute in authentic and effective leadership.

> Develop a strong sense of self-worth and surround yourself with positive role models who inspire you.

1
Nurturing the leader from the beginning

Growing and nurturing the leader within me

I understood from an early age that life has its challenges. To overcome challenges, I had to learn how to make the right choices at the right time. As I reminisce and trace back the origins of my formative years, I was developing my identity as an ambitious Māori woman leader with a fearless demeanour and a determined mindset. This unwavering attitude and tenacity have served me well, transforming me into a catalyst for change, shattering barriers and defying societal norms.

The Abraham children getting ready for Holy Communion and reconciliation at St Peters Church in Wairoa. Back row – Caroline, Julie & Hazel. Front row – Victor (baby of the family).

Nurturing the leader from the beginning

I am the eldest of my three siblings. It was only natural for me to assume the role of a leader and serve as a guiding example within my family. I consider myself incredibly fortunate to bear my grandmother's name Hazel, who was the daughter of Maramena Patangata and Pikitu Wanikau, and the wife of Tom Waikato. This legacy bestowed upon me by my parents holds a priceless intergenerational significance.

Although I initially did not fully grasp the immense potential lying within the knowledge and leadership skills that were inherently ingrained in me, serving others and assisting people allowed me to discover a better version of myself and nourish my inner strength. Throughout my life, I never expected that I would share with you the story of how I became brave and took courageous steps forward by simply pursuing my dreams. Reflecting upon my past and delving into the depths of my memories, I now realize that everyone experiences an insatiable urge to pursue something meaningful in life.

So, what drives you? What motivates you to start your day? Or are you simply existing, going through the motions, settling for mediocrity? Perhaps, you are seeking a higher salary, the perfect partner, or a fulfilling endeavour that brings warmth and joy to your life. I believe everyone has a choice, and it is perfectly all right to live without specific goals if that is what brings you contentment. If you are like me, an enthusiastic visionary, you refuse to accept anything less than what you truly deserve. Through my own experiences, I understand the importance of having a strategic plan and surrounding yourself with individuals who have already achieved success in the areas you aspire towards. The key to triumph lies in demonstrating an unwavering commitment to hard work, resilience, and never giving up when faced with challenges. Both of my parents have imparted valuable lessons to me, instilling the notion of not backing down and the importance of honesty. Honesty is a virtue we learn from our parents and the communities we find ourselves in as we navigate the path to maturity.

Defining an itch!

Let us start by defining what an itch is. An itch can be seen as a personal aspiration or desire that holds significance in your life. What does it mean to pursue an itch? And why is it such a common thread in my life and evident in other leaders as well? Well, it all boils down to our genetic makeup. As my family or *whānau*, would often remark, "It's in your genes, girl", "You're just like your mother", or "You're like your father." It is crucial to approach risks with caution and to embrace taking chances, especially when it comes to pursuing your dreams, or in other words, chasing an itch. For me, chasing an itch, started with me wanting to do something important with my life. It meant choosing a life path that allowed me to have options such as becoming a great person with a big heart, having the financial capabilities to travel and building an outstanding career of choice. It started with making good choices at school and learning how to be a great collaborator within my own family.

An itch can be seen as a symbolic representation of one's existence, which is likened to learning about your true purpose in life. Understanding what your true purpose is can led to immense levels of joy and excitement from living genuinely. To truly benefit from this chapter, it is crucial to be receptive to the idea of exploring concepts and thoughts from someone else's perspective, and to embark on a dual journey of self-discovery, reconnecting with oneself, and establishing a stronger connection with one's purpose by understanding your place in the world. From my point of view, as I recount my life's narrative, my dual journey serves to explore traditional knowledge freshly, mirroring my experiences of navigating both the Māori and Pākehā worlds. My intention, as you read, is to convey how my authentic encounters, encompassing the good, the bad, and the challenging moments, have contributed to my journey of empowerment and liberation from the constraints that once bound me.

The incredible opportunities that I have been granted through my life experiences have taken me on an extraordinary adventure. Along the way, various individuals have introduced me to different perspectives and approaches, some of which have been positive, while others have been quite challenging. However, these difficult moments have been instrumental in my personal growth, as I have been fortunate enough to have a wide range of experiences that have shaped me into becoming a strong and influential Māori woman leader, known as a *wahine toa*. This journey has allowed me to evolve and thrive in different aspects of life, becoming the best version of myself.

Letting go of past wrongs and embracing personal growth is not a simple task. However, with patience, time, a growth mindset, a positive attitude and the support of the people around you, and your family, you can navigate through the darkest phases of life. It is easier said than done, but as you embark on this journey with me, you will gradually discover your immense capabilities. The challenges you face will eventually transform into defining moments that shape your life. To move forward, it is crucial to reflect on the past as you step into the future. Perhaps you have heard the phrase 'fake it until you make it,' but I firmly believe in the concept of failing forward rather than falling back.

Chasing your itch (dreams)!

I have always passionately believed in pursuing my dreams. However, turning these dreams into reality has proven to be the most challenging aspect, filled with numerous obstacles and dilemmas that I have encountered throughout my eventful life. But when you meet Hazel, you encounter authenticity. There is no pretence, only genuine honesty, and a humble demeanour. I find myself thinking several steps ahead, and comprehending my thought process can be perplexing for others.

As a leader, it is important to listen to your intuition, that gut feeling and recognize the signals within yourself, the red and green lights that guide your decisions. Unfortunately, some individuals struggle to embrace their true selves, burdened by conflicting emotions and hidden motives. Through personal experience, if you choose to lead a double life, this can deeply harm your subjective wellbeing and alienate those close to you; thus intentionally hurting them in the process. However, by the time the damage is done, it is often too late to rectify the situation. If this occurs in your life, it is wiser to cut your losses rather than invest in a futile endeavour. Deciding to minimize losses and work towards a brighter future holds immense power. Ultimately, it demonstrates the ongoing growth within oneself, regardless of the cards that life has dealt. Inflicting harm upon others is firmly against my principles. Rather, we can derive valuable lessons from any wrongdoing, such as the strength of character and integrity we possess when faced with adversity. My dad consistently reminds me that if I cannot speak kind words, it is better to say nothing at all. Silence is a powerful tool and acts as an armoury which can save you from harm and allow you to feel inner peace by blocking out the noise that causes harm. This notion continuously motivates me to strive towards becoming an improved version of myself. Thank you Dad, for this invaluable lesson.

As I ponder upon my identity as Hazel, I question my drive for excellence and pushing the limits. To put it simply, achieving success in life brings about a sense of fulfilment. Who enjoys being on the losing side? No one, right? Every day presents itself as a gamble, but even in defeat, there lies the potential for personal growth and preparation for what lies ahead. The hardships we encounter can be repurposed into transformative experiences. Our perspective on life is shaped by what we see, feel, and experience. It is the negative moments that often drag us into a downward spiral. Therefore, it is crucial to be cautious of the overwhelming sensations that arise when our thoughts race, and instead, learn to utilise daily habits and commit to pursuing our passions to regain control. The importance of speaking kindly to ourselves and reframing our language cannot be underestimated. Strength arises from adversity. Without a plan, failure is inevitable. However, the wisdom gained from stumbling forward in life has greatly influenced the person I have become today.

Whakapapa (Genealogy and family connections)

From the very beginning, even before I arrived in this world, I was naturally inclined to curiosity. To comprehend my sense of belonging and connection to the land in Aotearoa New Zealand, I turn to my *whakapapa*, which holds the answers. *Whakapapa* is not easily translated, nor should it be limited to a mere family tree. To me, *whakapapa*, a Māori term for genealogy, emphasises the significant lineage of my ancestors on both my mother's and father's sides.

As I delve into my intricate *whakapapa*, I begin to understand why I have an inherent desire to pursue new experiences. The ancestors of both my mother and father were born leaders who aspired to create better lives for their families. They grew up in a time when Māori people faced hostility from society between the 1920s and 1950s. Success during that period meant owning a home, being a good spouse, and faithful churchgoer. However, my grandfather, Vic, challenged societal expectations by pursuing his passion for playing the E Flat Bass in a world-class brass band. He led with integrity and prioritized the wellbeing of his family.

Grandad Vic centred holding his E-Flat Bass was a member of the New Zealand Brass band and The World Championship Team (Holland)

I did not have the opportunity to know my grandmother, as her story is not as favourable. Grandad Vic overcame adversity through his active involvement in community sports and his advocacy for the rights of labourers. He always showed love and support to his children, especially my father. These strong role models demonstrated that true leadership involves selfless, unconditional love and service to both family and community. Their examples established the vital foundations necessary for building relationships with others, especially close ones. Coming from a family with various talents, I set out to make my mark by being an exemplary student and excelling in my education.

My mother is of Māori descent. Her lineage can be traced back to the *atua*, or Māori gods, and her remarkable qualities, abilities, and strong connection to the land and environment are evident in our Waikato *whānau rangatira* (chief, leader) ancestry. Our familial ties originate from various tribes, including Ngāti Awa, Ngāti Tūwharetoa, Ngāi Tūhoe, Whakatōhea, and Ngāti Rangitihi. The women who raised my mother were incredibly strong individuals, having grown up on the *marae* (ancestral home), under the watchful guidance of their grandmothers. These elders possessed deep ties to *te ao Māori*, or the Māori world, and were deeply rooted in *Mātauranga Māori, tikanga Māori* (cultural customs, practices), and Māori values.

On my father's side, my *whakapapa* takes me on a fascinating journey through time. Our ancestral line can be traced back to Victor Toussaint Joseph Abraham, a French Jewish Chef. He had an ardent passion for food and luxury, which eventually led him away from Buckingham Palace because of his relationship with his second wife. Emma originated from the Kingston River Thames in London and arrived in colonial New Zealand during the early 1900s.

My paternal grandmother, Gladys Downey, had Irish ancestry whose ancestors braved the journey to New Zealand during the colonial period. They settled in Central Otago, located in the South Island, where they worked as miners and rabbiters. It is worth noting that my great-grandfather played a significant role in the community by constructing the Catholic Church in Queenstown. He now rests in peace within the central cemetery of the town.

The common thread that runs through the histories of both sets of my ancestors is their unwavering determination and resilience. They faced many challenges but never gave up, showing me the importance of perseverance in life.

The role of parents in nurturing leadership within the family

During my childhood, I was fortunate to be surrounded by immense affection and unwavering support from both my father and my mother's extended family. My father, being compassionate and considerate, made a conscious decision to relocate us closer to my mother's *whānau*, resulting in a shift from the bustling city to the serene countryside. Our residence on Udy Street in Petone was a haven nestled by the beach. Petone, a small settlement within Lower Hutt, was renowned for its working-class community. Eventually, we moved once again, this time to Wainuiomata. However, during the 1980s, Wainuiomata was unfortunately regarded as a financially disadvantaged area within Wellington.

My father's unwavering devotion to our mother was clear in his actions. His selflessness drove him to prioritize the wellbeing of his family more than anything else. The love and care that a parent has for their children can undoubtedly mould and shape one's character. Interestingly, the depth of love shared between individuals can occasionally lead them to act out of character, sometimes with devastating consequences overall. As a leader, it is vital to consistently do what is morally right, maintaining integrity in every decision and action undertaken. Mindfulness of our leadership actions can truly expose both our human flaws and exceptional talents.

As a child, I observed the importance of having a strong character and maintaining integrity to achieve your dreams. My dad was determined to provide us with a home, which led him to make the difficult decision of leaving his family and taking care of his own family. He had good intentions in moving forward with mum and us to Wairoa, creating a compromise to maintain peace with our mother while also offering opportunities for our family to thrive.

This situation placed a significant amount of responsibility on my young shoulders, as the oldest and firstborn. Early on, I learned how to navigate the system and understood what motivated people. I quickly realized that if I wanted something, I had to work hard for it. For example, if I wanted to get the top in my class for all my exams, I had to do more work than the other students with my study. Despite the challenges we faced during our childhood, I discovered that effective communication and self-discipline were key to overcoming difficult situations. This taught me the steps for success and the intrinsic satisfaction that comes with it.

6 KEY TIPS FROM CHAPTER 1:

1. Mindset and a go-getter attitude are developed in early childhood years.
2. Cultural identity develops based on surroundings and influence in the early years.
3. Life experiences and people influence your views of your self-image and self-worth.
4. Self-limiting beliefs prevent you from reaching your potential. Negative experiences contribute to self-limiting beliefs.
5. Self-limiting beliefs can impact on relationships and need to be changed.
6. Do not accept someone else's projected feelings and opinions of you.

Epigenetics across a lifespan can be altered by toxic environments, social surroundings, and stressful life circumstances. Critical to building a strong sense of self-worth involves surrounding yourself with positive role models which is essential for personal growth and well-being. Here are some steps that could be taken away by you in cultivating a strong sense of self-worth and creating a positive support system:

1. *Self-Reflection:*

    - Reflect on your strengths, values, and accomplishments.
    - Identify areas where you excel and the qualities that make you unique.
    - Recognize and appreciate your achievements, no matter how small.

2. *Set Healthy Boundaries:*

- Establish and communicate clear boundaries to protect your well-being.
- Learn to say no to activities or relationships that compromise your values.
- Prioritize self-care and prioritize your mental and emotional health.

3. *Positive Affirmations:*

- Practice positive self-talk and affirmations.
- Challenge negative thoughts and replace them with empowering statements.
- Reinforce positive beliefs about yourself regularly.

4. *Surround Yourself with Positivity:*

- Identify and spend time with people who uplift and support you.
- Seek friends, family, or colleagues who have a positive influence.
- Distance yourself from individuals who bring negativity or toxicity into your life.

5. *Seek Positive Role Models:*

- Identify individuals who inspire and motivate you.
- Look for role models who embody qualities you admire and aspire to develop.
- Listen to your mentor(s) experiences and take from their stories how they handled challenges.

6. ***Engage in Personal Development***:

- Continuously invest in your personal development.
- Attend workshops, read books, or take courses that contribute to your growth.
- Set specific goals for self-improvement and track your progress.

7. ***Cultivate a Support System:***

- Build a network of supportive friends, family, or mentors.
- Share your goals and aspirations with them.
- Seek advice and guidance from those who have your best interests at heart.

8. ***Celebrate Achievements:***

- Acknowledge and celebrate your accomplishments.
- Set realistic goals and reward yourself when you achieve them.
- Use positive reinforcement to boost your self-esteem.

9. ***Mindfulness and Gratitude***:

- Practice mindfulness to stay present and appreciate the current moment.
- Cultivate gratitude by focusing on the positive aspects of your life.
- Keep a gratitude journal to record daily moments of appreciation.

10. ***Contribute to Others:***

- Engage in acts of kindness and contribute to the well-being of others.
- Volunteering and helping others can enhance your sense of purpose.
- Build positive connections by being a source of support for those around you.
- Remember, developing a strong sense of self-worth is a continuous process. Surrounding yourself with positivity and positive role models contributes significantly to your growth, resilience, and overall well-being.

Wairoa Intermediate School 1989 Form 1

2

The importance of education and educational experiences in cultivating leadership skills

School was a place where I not only succeeded but thrived, as I was enthusiastic about learning and excelling in all areas of my life. However, with success comes responsibility, and I knew my choices could impact my friendships. I surrounded myself with like-minded individuals who shared my academic interests, which was a wise decision. I was confident in my choices, and I knew I did not want to engage in the same activities as other students who engaged in drinking or dating. Everyone has the freedom to choose their path, but I was determined to stay true to myself and my values.

I was academically successful in school and avoided parties as they did not benefit me. I was innately aware of my inherent leadership qualities passed down through my *whakapapa*. However, I observed that Māori students and families suffered financially and in impoverished conditions. Some teachers were unconsciously racist and biased towards Māori students, preferring Pākehā kids because they came across as more obedient and less resistant to change. Many Pākehā teachers failed to understand the impact of intergenerational cultural trauma on Māori educational success. I witnessed firsthand Pākehā and international teachers dehumanizing Māori students. It was unacceptable.

The importance of education and educational experiences

Wairoa Primary school pupil Hazel Abraham is one of the artists who's w[ork] was selected for the annual Dominion Newspaper Art Exhibition. School[s in] the paper's circulation enter the competition and two are usually select[ed per] district. Hazel's successful painting was of Maui when he fished-up the N[orth] Island. She is invited to see the exhibition in Wairarapa but it will be in W[airoa] next year.

Hazel with her Standard Four teacher, Mr Roger Mole at Wairoa Primary School.

The importance of education and educational experiences

In the 1990s, I attended Wairoa Intermediate School where we experienced a challenging year with a high turnover of 11 teachers. Many of the students, mainly of Māori descent, faced difficult circumstances associated with gangs and poverty. In class, I spoke up when my teacher racially abused and profiled my friend. Another friend, being rather more assertive, took things a step further by strongly and derogatively telling the teacher to leave. The class erupted into a state of chaos, all hell broke loose.

On another occasion, a senior Pākehā teacher ordered trouble-causing students to put their heads into their desks and slammed their desktops down on the three boys. There were no consequences for this teacher, except for a stern reprimand from one of the boys' mothers, who was a Māori schoolteacher. No one stood up against this atrocity. As young teenagers, often you choose not to confront elders for fear of rejection and embarrassment. This incident taught me the importance of maintaining integrity, even when emotions ran high.

The influence of social circles on the evolution of a leader

My childhood was filled with a mix of positive, negative, and challenging experiences. The people we surround ourselves with will influence who we become. During my early years, I gravitated toward friends who excelled academically. I vividly recall expressing my desire to escape my circumstances to my Rangi cousins. Little did I know then that this unwavering determination would later drive me to serve my community and strive for better change. The feeling of achievement and educational success motivated me, triggering a dopamine response that pushed me to keep pursuing my goals and dreams. This mindset allowed me to navigate through New Zealand's mainstream education system and accomplish feats that surprised even my teachers. Believing in oneself from a young age is crucial, as is growing up in a loving and supportive environment. Each step forward in our journey requires continuous learning and resilience to keep falling forward despite setbacks. Even during moments when my inner voice struggled, winning in the classroom provided validation and reassurance. It is important to remember that setbacks do not define us, and there will always be someone to lend a hand and encourage us to pursue our aspirations.

I think you must have a fire in your belly to push yourself further and not compare yourself to others. As a kid, I loved competing to be the best in Mathematics, English, and Science. I loved having my name called at assemblies and getting an award for 100% on my maths times tables. What you need to watch out for is people who are jealous of your growth and want to steal things from you by saying negative things about yourself and sending vibrations you are not good enough. Everyone has grit and determination to do well in life, but from an incredibly young age, my parents, through their hard work and family planning taught me to be the best at putting priorities first and family should always come first. This meant that the best times we spent together were swimming and camping on the beach in Mahia. Life was effortless and the calming effect of the sea beach does wonders for one's *wairua* (soul, spirit of a person) but also in terms of community building.

From here I learned as a child that the best place for me was being one with nature and having common shared beliefs and values as a community. To grow your community, you must be prepared to put the effort into your family and that begins with you. What we learn in childhood has a flow-on effect on how we overcome loss, defeat, and challenges. For me to become a winner I also had to overcome challenges and learn the hard way that meant falling forward.

6 KEY TIPS FROM CHAPTER 2:

1. School is a great place to build your character and cultivate skills in building your self-concept.

2. School is where you learn to become successful. Teachers can influence your children's desire to achieve higher at school.

3. Friendship circles can have a positive or negative impact on children's confidence to find their way in life.

4. School is a safe place for some children to get away from negative influencers.

5. Developing your curiosity for learning can be influenced and shaped by the school environment.

6. Learning to show up for others is influenced by the friends who surround you at school and in your family circle.

> In the tapestry of lived experiences, the adolescent period builds the fundamental cornerstone for life's purpose and development of leadership skills, attributes, and practices.

3

Inspiring dreams through familial support and encouragement from educators

Strengthening the development of life purpose, passions, and interests in adolescence

Understanding what your talents are and developing these is vital for being successful in life. Critical to your success are the role models you have to guide you on your life journey. A role model is someone you look up to as a good example and who is worthy of imitating. In my case, the role models I looked up to had influenced me as a teenager. The strong male role models I had were my dad and his brother, Uncle Pat. They showed me what it was to walk with honour and have integrity. Likewise, the strong women I looked up to were fierce and relentless but also gentle and nurturing. One of my greatest challenges I had ever faced was leaving home at 14 years old. When I reflect on Hazel then, she was independent and full of passion. Not afraid to take risks and doing what she wanted to do. How many teenagers do you know just leave home, uproot, and change their whole environment? In the next five years, living away from home would serve me well as I started my university years living in the halls of residence in Palmerston North. So, in hindsight, I was being guided by my ancestors, searching for a better way of life through my passion to learn and dream big.

With the help of my dad, who I consider being one of the most important role models and greatest encouragers in my life. Dad showed me how to turn up in life, take the knocks we face in life, survive extreme challenges, and bounce back stronger than before from upsets in life. Dad showed me that with hard work, and being disciplined, you can be a successful person. What success looked like from my dad was setting time and energy aside in caring for his family, providing a roof over our heads, and being selfless and unconditional in loving his children and mum. We never went without. Although times got hard, Dad showed his skills in hunting and gathering food. As the leader of our family, he understood his purpose was to take care of the household and be a family person. These leadership traits were common with him and Uncle Pat. Both were successful in their way of being and leading authentically with purpose. They were taught the difference between right and wrong by their father, Grandad Vic, to stick by their family and do the right thing. These two proud and stoic men were not only leaders, but they showered their families with love and gave willingly of their time to their communities.

Such happy memories make me reminiscent of the fun times we had together even more when Uncle moved from Paraparaumu to Otaki. Visiting Uncle Pat at the Paraparaumu Hotel and Fielding Hotel was so much fun. Dad worked as the right-hand man to Uncle Pat, who had the license to be a publican with the breweries. Uncle would always shower us with treats and gifts. As his three favourite nieces, Victor wasn't around then, Uncle Pat would walk us into the kitchen chiller to help ourselves to what ever we wanted. I remember walking out with an entire pavlova, and that was such a great time. It felt like you were in heaven, and all your wishes had come true, all at once, and you could visually imagine seeing three sets of eyes looking at all the delicious sweets and treats. Growing up in bars was second nature for us kids. We would help our mum with her cleaning job at the Ferry Hotel and collecting the cans and tidying up after rugby functions for Tapuae in Wairoa.

Uncle Pat was our *Rangatira* (chief) of the Abraham family and I had an extraordinarily strong connection with him as a child. When Uncle Pat was diagnosed with cancer, it was a full blow to the family. Uncle Pat was due to have an operation, so dad drove the family in the Ford Falcon to Palmerston North Hospital. Uncle Pat was all that we knew of Dad's family and seeing Uncle Pat in the hospital showed a sense of urgency for him to maintain the family bond. Dad and Uncle Pat were skilled in the old way. They were skilled by their father and taught the family values of integrity, honesty and living with honour. Honour is what a man has, and it can be easily taken or thrown away by doing wrong to others. As the head of his family, Uncle Pat showed me how a man should be to his family, to be selfless and enduring, and to treat women well. He taught me the spirit of fighting like a tiger, to never say die, and reinforced to me that I could be whatever I wanted to be. These values of love and family were also strongly entrenched in my psyche and were firmly planted in my dad's philosophy of teaching his own children on how to be caring and kind people in life and help other people within your community whilst grounding us kids to never ever settle for mediocrity or allow people to treat us with disrespect. My father and Uncle had great charisma and *mana* (prestige and supernatural force in a person). As *tuakana* (eldest sibling) and *teina* (youngest sibling), brothers in arms, they were men of great honour, who lived by their strong family values that were generationally taught by their father who grew up in the early colonial years into the start of the twentieth century in Aotearoa New Zealand. I believed that if I became the most educated person, I could take care of myself, and I would not need to rely on someone else to financially support me. Not only were they inspiring a new generation of Abraham family members, but they were also smashing barriers to the intermarriage of Māori women.

So, during Uncle Pat's last holiday to Wairoa, Uncle asked me if I could go on holiday with him and Aunty. Mum would have rather I stayed at home and got a job. I was 12 years old at the time, Mum being the direct and strong woman she was, sent me marching down to the local dairy to ask for a job. Unintentionally, the green-eyed monster can be disguised as coming out of those you love or actively work with. Sometimes, without knowing why things happen, it is important to be aware of the red flags that go off within you. This internal alert mechanism must not be ignored inside of you. Easier said than done. But listening to one's warning system, that is the gut instinct you have when something is not quite right, is often a telling feature or characteristic of your *tipuna* (elder/s) wisdom indicating to watch out for this person or situation you are in.

Getting my first job down at the local Maclean Street dairy in Wairoa I was paid $5 per hour and made $20 for a solid four hours. In a year, I saved my first $1000. I did not have a plan to grow my savings as I was so focused on getting a university education. I can remember the sense of pride in serving customers and having a sense of self-worth from someone trusting in me to deal with their business. Not only was I serving customers, but I also learned to cook fish and chips. For me, these early experiences in the workforce allowed me to grow and become more independent. I did this job for less than a year before I left home in Wairoa to live with my aunt in Otaki.

Before I share more of my journey in leaving home at 14 years of age, let us look at several questions about how life's purpose can influence you in chasing that itch:

How do you know what your life purpose is?

Having direction and understanding of what your life's purpose is, can bring meaning into your existence and serve as the catalyst for the driving force behind chasing your dreams and aspirations. When you are an adolescent, you are developing your ideas and thoughts of oneself. The people you are surrounded by can influence your moral standings, spiritual beliefs, and sense of self-worth. According to Yukhymenko-Lescroart and Sharma (2023), your purpose can be altruistic, meaning the unselfish gift of selflessness, of serving others above oneself. In my early years, I already knew that my dream was to go to university, leave home and spread my wings. Therefore, discovering your purpose involves identifying and acknowledging your unique talents and utilising them to make a positive impact on society. Having goals, ambitions, and a sense of direction can contribute to a purposeful life and better health and wellbeing (Yukhymenko-Lescroart & Sharma, 2023).

Every individual's purpose is distinctive and unique; what resonates as your calling may not align with that of others. A commonly used definition of purpose in life was provided by Damon et al. (2003), who defined purpose as: "a stable and generalized intention to accomplish something that is at once meaningful to the self and of consequence to the world beyond self" (p. 121). One's purpose is not set in stone and can evolve in tandem with shifting priorities and personal growth. I know from experience that my life's purpose has been reimagined to bring more realness and meaning to my life. This also has included looking inwards at myself and working on me. Awakening to and having an awareness of purpose has a direct correlation to subjective wellbeing (subjective happiness, life satisfaction) (Yukhymenko-Lescroart & Sharma, 2023). Contemplating one's life purpose often brings about introspective questions such as: what defines me? Where is my place in the world? When do I experience true satisfaction?

A transition point - Leaving home to follow my life purpose

The impetus for setting off was I could see an opportunity to gain experience and start a new life away from home. I learnt from my mother how to be tough, bold, and hardworking. Mum was a straight shooter who worked hard all her life and was raised in a Māori way. Looking after the *whānau* and the elders was part in parcel of who she was. Supporting the community through growing gardens was a key strength of my mother. Being self-sufficient with what you have and working hard are two gems or green lights that are important parts of my leadership approach. When my dad asked me if I wanted to live away in Otaki, I jumped at the opportunity. I did not give one thought about how this would hurt my siblings and affect them. All I could think of was getting away from my mother.

Inspiring dreams through familial support

So, leaving home was quite a challenging time, but exciting. I understood taking risks was part of life. I honestly enjoyed being in Otaki as I got to try new things and solidify my education pursuit of chasing that itch to go to university. At school, I excelled and was streamed into the top class for forms four, and five. I enjoyed being with the top achievers as we had this unparalleled sense of competitive spirit. I learned that going the extra mile and doing more than enough would edge me closer to my dream. I did the hard yards and applied myself religiously to my studies, attending extra support classes to advance my learning. What teenager is into bookwork and avoids parties? Well, that was me. I had an internal drive within me. I wanted more in life, and I did not want to end up in a labouring job in the gardens, living week by week for a pay cheque that was weather dependant. I knew from an early age that parties and, of course, boys would come along once I had captured my itch.

Another powerful moment of living in Otaki was seeing the world around me, which differed from little Wairoa. Otaki was an hour to Wellington and Palmerston North. The coastal town was very white in population and had a rich abundance of businesses. I felt a bit out of place sometimes and again, here are those red flags going off inside. Awkwardness is a state of being put out of your comfort zone. A feeling of being challenged. It is necessary to feel challenged, but not if it makes you feel awkward and out of balance.

I got to do a lot of firsts at college, like being a student leader of our school council group and going to the school ball. The group of friends I associated with were some of the most intellectual and bright cookies I had ever met. Andrew, I could swear he would have become the Prime Minister of New Zealand. He knew more than the teachers and was teaching us Statistics and Accounting. Lauren and Michele were so kind and had that whiff of innocence. They were religious and strong in their faith. I wanted to make new friends, so I tagged along to lunchtime bible sessions. Yes, it was a revelation, and it felt like a safe place to be until I settled and made new friends. What I say about these two school friends is their underlying faith in God.

Hazel at 16 years old getting ready for her School Ball at Cousin Mike and Chris's home at Otaki Beach

Inspiring dreams through familial support

Otaki College Form Six Homeroom

Otaki College Netball

Otaki College School Council

Otaki College Form Seven

Hazel getting ready for the School Ball

Hazel and the team at Eithne's home for pre drinks before the School Ball. Back row – Andre, Lauren's plus one, Andrew, Stuart. Front row – Helen, Anita, Bianca, Lauren, Eithne, Hazel

I had a great friend who I felt right at home with at Otaki. Brenda was the social one, and I loved staying with her at her mum's place who also was my English teacher in sixth form. Helen was the best English teacher that I had in my secondary schooling time. I loved how she taught William Shakespeare's, Othello. Brenda and I would often have a lot of laughs, drink a little wine, and share our views on life. Brenda left home and wanted to explore. I will always remember her wild and free spirit. A gifted poet who had the itch to chase the university of life. Lastly, there was Eithne. A beautiful Irish girl with whom I did most things with until I headed off to university in Palmerston North and she went to Victoria University in Wellington. Eithne's mum was a fierce woman. Her godly advice was if you met a boy after three dates, get rid of him. He needed to commit. Tess was a staunch catholic, so it was natural for me and Eithne to go to church together and go through confirmation. Eithne and I spent most of our free time studying and going to swimming club. Seeing the joy in Eithne's eye when she beat me in a race sent a racing roar through her mum's face. Sometimes in life, you must let others win for their benefit. Although I lost, I had fallen forward by becoming a better person. Something to remember is winning sometimes means losing, so others get to feel that joy of success.

As a teenager, I was so dedicated to my studies that I gave up playing netball to concentrate on studying for fifth form school certificate. I also took on a weekend part-time job to help fund my itch to go to university. I enjoyed working for the Chinese market gardeners because of their hard work ethic. I saved for two years which paid for my first year at university. What I can say is the Chinese love to work and make money. They were fair bosses, and I learnt nothing comes from life if you do not work hard. I also owed them a lot for taking a chance on me as a 15-year-old teenager. Barbara and Murray gave me holiday work while I was still at college. I enjoyed the customer engagement and getting my hands dirty with cleaning vegetables, and repacking hundreds of carrots and potatoes into smaller kilo bags which were only 900grams. I also looked forward to most finishing times because my bosses always had a lot of jobs to give me to do. To them, time was money. I worked long hours from 8 am to 5 pm for $45.00. So, the first year I saved $1800 that went to my university fund. I also won a Masonic Lodge scholarship. The combined savings of the last three years of my time in Otaki allowed me to get into my first year at Massey University in Palmerston North.

My maths teacher sticks out the most to me at Otaki College. He was Pākehā, an astute and tall man who was rather undermining towards me. He projected towards me that I could not pass School Certificate (SC) Mathematics. See, SC is an education qualification that was designed for secondary school students who were in fifth form to assess their understanding of the curriculum. This qualification was a stepping stone to moving into the next year's level. When someone challenges me, I fight back, and I made it my mission to show my maths teacher that he was wrong about his perception of me being successful. My teacher's little understanding of cultural concepts and *te ao Māori* was rather clear in his prophesising of my lack of ability to pass SC in the fourth form. I did extra classes and attended Saturday workshops sessions as preparation for SC. I had no choice but to have to sit there and put up with my maths teacher's dry sense of humour and sabotaging thoughts of my ability to succeed as a Māori student to the side. With all the extra effort, I passed SC Mathematics in fourth form. It was the greatest feeling as in those days New Zealand's education system unfairly disadvantaged Māori and had scaling as a mechanism to make students fit inside of a bell curve formula. What this time showed me is that falling forward means I am closer to my goal than I realised, and with consistent discipline and effort, I will be successful.

The impact of Māori elders in mentoring of rangatahi (youth) to follow their dreams

Another important time in Otaki was meeting my *whangai* mother, Ramahora Broughton. Through her daughter Nikola, we became remarkably close to each other. Nikola was Māori and was a good friend I had while I was at Otaki College. We did many trips together and shared many special occasions as friends. Nikola was the organist at church as well, so on Saturdays and sometimes Sundays I would attend mass with my aunty. Nikola was also my sponsor for confirmation into the Catholic church. We would talk late at night when I stayed over and visit. Nikola showed me how grace and beauty go hand in hand and was successful in being a winner in a beauty pageant whilst working as a real estate agent. I also learned from Nikola to never give up on one's studies. She had to return to school because she did not pass her papers. Considering this, hard work shone through, and Nikola could pass her papers.

Hazel and Nikola (Sponsor) at her confirmation with Father

I enjoyed spending time with Ramahora and Nanna Agnes, as they were like nannies to me. These staunch Māori women were standing on their own two feet in their beautiful home in Te Horo. What Ramahora and Nanna did for me was guide me through challenging times and moments I faced in life. The most important gift Ramahora taught me was to be gentle with myself and be gentle to my mother. They both introduced me to the Māori Women's Welfare League, where I felt right at home. I went to National Conference as a delegate and was surrounded by successful Māori women in business. I wanted to be just like these Māori women, in charge and successful. That was to be an itch I would chase later in life.

Hazel being presented flowers for graduating with her Diploma from Massey University College of Education by Ramahora, President of the Tararua Otaki Māori Women's Welfare League

Inspiring dreams through familial support

**Hazel with Maria and Nanna Agnes life members
of the Māori Women's Welfare League**

So, after three years of living in Otaki, it became apparent that I was heading in a new direction from my family in Otaki. I had been accepted into university, and I was going to live in the halls of residence. I was glad to get away and be released into the wider world.

Your life purpose is entangled with strengthening your identity of self, identity with family, and identity with community during adolescence. Part of living your life's purpose is learning to identify what your gift is, identify your talents, and discerning what one is going to do with such gifts and talents. You must train and use your talents. It takes guts to fail and lose in life. You must get up and try every day and set your sights high.

If you want to get something you never had, you must take risks and be open to new views. You must learn to never hold back and to take a chance on things you want because you do not want to be reflecting on your life and be saying to yourself, I did not take a risk and missed the opportunity to chase your itch. Failing is inevitable in life. What I share with you about failing is to embrace losing because it means you are one step closer to realising your dream. I had belief and prayed. As a teenager leaving home, I would catch a break and realise my true potential to shine bright like a diamond. So, whatever that itch is you are chasing, that is proof you are growing and moving in that direction. What my family, and particularly my Uncle Pat and Dad have taught me is anything good, you can have it. You just must claim it and reach back and help someone else along. So, make sure you teach one and lead one person in your life to fulfil the truest expression of themselves as a human being!

6 KEY TIPS FROM CHAPTER 3:

1. Your life's purpose can change and evolve because of different transitioning points in life.
2. Watch out for the red flags, disruptions to your progress, and limits put on you by people. Be mindful that when looking through the eyes of people who discourage you and belittle you, it is better to remove these people from your life.
3. Watch out for the green flags, as opportunities come all the time. You just have to realise this when it happens. Take risks, it opens the door to better opportunities.
4. Challenge yourself to break glass ceilings and rise above self-limiting beliefs.
5. There is only one of you in the world, so develop your talents so the world can experience what you offer.
6. Call out bullying and institutional racism. It can impact on people's wellbeing and the educational success of Māori navigating mainstream education in New Zealand.

This chapter introduces the idea of how the early years can shape your destiny and begin your journey in life. The importance of family support and role modelling of family values is shared in my story, and a synopsis of how the statement above can be interpreted and applied by people on their journey of discovery. Here is the breakdown of what the *whakataukī* (proverb) in the tapestry of lived experiences means to me:

1. ***Tapestry of Lived Experiences***:

    - The metaphor of a tapestry implies a weaving together of various life experiences, creating a rich and intricate whole.
    - Lived experiences encompass a range of moments, both positive and challenging, that contribute to personal growth.

2. ***Adolescent Period as Fundamental Cornerstone***:

    - The specific focus on the adolescent period suggests that the formative years of youth have a profound impact on shaping an individual's identity.
    - This period is a foundational cornerstone, showing that experiences during adolescence lay the groundwork for future development.

3. ***Life Purpose Development***:

    - The statement proposes that the adolescent period is influential in the formation of life's purpose.
    - During adolescence, individuals often explore their values, passions, and aspirations, contributing to the development of a sense of purpose.

4. ***Leadership Skills, Attributes, and Practices***:

    - The assertion that the adolescent period is crucial for the development of leadership skills, attributes, and practices suggests that these formative years lay the groundwork for leadership qualities.

- Interactions, challenges, and personal growth during adolescence may contribute to the acquisition of skills like communication, resilience, and decision-making.

5. ***Foundational Nature of Experiences***:

- The use of 'fundamental cornerstone' emphasizes the significance of experiences during adolescence as the building blocks for a person's future.
- The notion is that these experiences serve as a foundation upon which later aspects of life, including purpose and leadership, are constructed.

6. ***Continuous Development***:

- The idea of the adolescent period as a fundamental cornerstone implies that the impact is enduring.
- The experiences during this time are not viewed as isolated events, but as part of an ongoing process of development.

In summary, the adolescent period, within the broader tapestry of lived experiences, is a critical phase that lays the foundation for life's purpose and the development of leadership skills. It underscores the importance of understanding and valuing the experiences and challenges faced during adolescence as they contribute significantly to the fabric of one's life journey.

> Authentic leadership stems from the lived experiences that shape our character, reminding us that every challenge we face is a stepping stone toward becoming a resilient leader.

ptart
4
The university years of experimentation and living my purpose

Being discipline, focused and committed to learning

I was following my purpose in life as a young adult trying to find my way in the world. My university years would prove to be a transformative journey of intention and the invaluable importance of cultivating habits. As part of embarking on my academic voyage, I possessed an unwavering focus fuelled by my desire to maximise my potential. Armed with my ambition and a thirst for knowledge, I set forth on a path that would unravel the secrets of the universe. However, I soon realised that merely having intention was not enough.

Intentions are like seeds planted in fertile soil; they hold immense potential but require diligent nurturing to blossom into reality. It was through the power of habit that I reaped the rewards of my intentions. I forged a routine that intertwined seamlessly with my university life, ensuring that every day brought me closer to my goals. I created habits that would help me with my intentions. As a young Māori student, I had always possessed an innate talent for education, blessed with a natural curiosity and an insatiable thirst for knowledge.

Growing up in Wairoa, I faced numerous challenges and obstacles on my educational journey. It was through the formation of habits that I found the key to success. A habit is a learned routine behaviour that could either be healthy, unhealthy, or neutral. Understanding the power of healthy habits, I set out to cultivate ones that would lead me toward educational achievement.

With unwavering discipline and self-determination, I embraced my love for school and learning. Education became my creative field, where I flourished and soared to new heights. My dedication and commitment to my studies brought me early triumphs, as I proudly became the recipient of the prestigious Joanna Wolf Dux Award at Wairoa Primary School.

The university years of experimentation and living my purpose

Hazel and Terry. Celebrating her achievements as the top student, Dux of Wairoa Primary (1989) at home in Wairoa.

Developing good habits to enjoy educational success in secondary school

As I progressed in my secondary school years at Wairoa and Otaki College, I continued to excel academically. My hard work, zeal, diligence, and perseverance were recognized when I was placed in the top classes amongst my peers. But my educational journey did not end there. My community service and school accomplishments caught the attention of the Masonic Lodge, who awarded me a substantial education scholarship over three years.

Reflecting upon my success, I realised that more than just personal attributes were at play. The habits they had diligently cultivated played a significant role in my achievements. The friendships I had nurtured and the supportive environment that I had created were equally responsible for my growth mindset.

I firmly believed that dreaming big is essential for anyone aspiring to pursue higher education. Starting early and envisioning a future filled with possibilities is paramount. Surrounded by one's close-knit group of school friends, family members and the dedicated teachers at both my colleges, I found the support and inspiration I needed to keep reaching for the stars.

I had recognised the reality that not everyone may have role models within their families who have pursued a university education. However, rather than feeling discouraged, I saw this as an opportunity to find my community, my own "mob," as I fondly called it. A mob is a group of like-minded individuals who share their aspirations and understand each other's journey. Finding solace and strength in this newfound community, I pushed forward, fearlessly embracing the challenges that lay ahead. Through my healthy habits, determination, and the unwavering support of my "mob," I ensured that my dreams of attending university would become a reality.

As a young child and teenager, I was deeply influenced by the experiences of my family and the life I witnessed around me. These experiences fuelled my determination to become someone and live a meaningful life. I was motivated to avoid working in the gardens and engaging in laborious jobs, as I observed the tireless efforts of my *whānau* and mother in the gardens at Te Teko. They would wake up early at 6am, toil until around 4pm, and persevere through all types of weather. My *whānau* knew how to *mahi* (work) and showed dedication and commitment to doing a good job for their bosses.

The university years of experimentation and living my purpose

Choosing pathways for university

Before ultimately deciding to pursue a career in teaching, I explored four different pathways. One of them involved my childhood memories of visiting Uncle Pat, which sparked an interest in hotel management. I considered becoming an accountant or a lawyer. Delving into my father's *whakapapa*, I discovered that our Abraham family had a strong background in law and in being union delegates fighting for labourer's rights. I had chosen the relevant academic subjects that would grant me admission into university programmes related to these fields. However, during my final years at Otaki College, my enthusiasm for Economics and Accounting waned because of the absence of a teacher and having to study through correspondence.

The strength of my decision played a crucial role in my success during my school years and as I embarked on a university education journey. Decisions hold immense significance as they can either dismantle or improve one's life. I can vividly recall the thrill and excitement I experienced when I received school bursary and successfully passed the university entrance (UE) examination. See I never passed School C English and Bursary English. But it didn't matter as I got enough grades to get across the line. That was four Cs and a D. The previous year, I had already been accepted into teacher's training college in Palmerston North. I had made all the preparations for what I considered the most important year of my life. It meant living independently, away from my parents, and having the freedom to make my own choices. In February 1996, Aunty June kindly dropped me off at Blair Tennant, the renowned student accommodation for trainee teachers. Blair Tennant played a significant role in the lives of aspiring educators and was conveniently situated across from the Fitz Pub.

Students at Massey University in Palmerston North had a special connection to The Fitz Pub. It was a symbol of our university experience, where we often spotted fellow students strolling around in their cozy swandri and aertex shirts. It became our designated meeting spot for gathering with friends. I must confess that we frequented the Fitz after completing our assignments. After all, who would want to miss the opportunity to purchase an entire tray of vodka and cokes for a mere $20.00? During those days, four of us could share a tray on a weekday.

Hazel and Sharon celebrating at the FITZ Pub. The local pub for Massey University students

The university years of experimentation and living my purpose

**Hazel and Sharon
in the square at Palmerston North**

My enthusiasm for learning was palpable. When you are in your element, your true self instinctively gravitates towards what is best for you. While I enjoyed all my classes, I had a particular fondness for the Treaty of Waitangi paper, which was taught on the Turitea campus. It is worth noting that the lecturer of this course, Professor Mason Durie was a leading Māori academic who was promoting the need for Māori advancement in New Zealand. Massey University proved to be an excellent environment for both learning and personal growth. I thoroughly enjoyed my experiences as a student teacher, venturing out to various schools. Naturally, my goal was to become a principal, so pursuing my undergraduate degree aligned perfectly with this aspiration. However, it must be acknowledged that the university setting did not always cater well to Māori students. Most of my Māori friends were enrolled in the secondary Physical Education programme, while other Māori students I knew participated in the Māori immersion programmes.

I thoroughly enjoyed my time living in the halls of residence at Blair Tennant, which provided an opportunity for me to reconnect with my school friends from Wairoa College. Among them, a few had chosen the path of becoming educators. There was a strong sense of camaraderie among us as we vowed to watch out for one another. When we gathered all the Māori students together, it was an absolute blast. Those were the moments when I truly let loose. I vividly recall my first experience of overindulging in homemade vodka, resulting in an unfortunate bout of vomiting. You see, I never back down from a challenge, and David had dared me to compete shot for shot. After we polished off a case of wine, we delved into the homemade brew. Alas, that marked the end of my night. My compassionate friend had to chase after me to prevent me from venturing outside in her moon boot. These experiences taught me the importance of having fun while also maintaining a balance with my studies. It became evident that having a supportive group of friends was crucial to keeping me on track. When studying at university, many temptations to go partying arise. However, I recognized that if I wanted to achieve my dreams, I had to make sacrifices and needed to stay disciplined and committed to my academic goals. With four years still ahead of me, I had to ensure that partying did not consume all my time.

Constantly seeking bargains and opportunities for personal growth, I enthusiastically joined the student executive committee at Massey University College of Education. I had heard that this was a fantastic endeavour, promising not only a good time at lively parties but also the enticing offers of leadership kickbacks. The toga and student stampede parties I attended were nothing short of wild, crazy, and fun. In the late 1990s in Palmerston North, it was customary to roam around with a box of steines, vodka cruisers, vaults, and purple goannas. I even dared to participate in the funnels. However, I was not afraid to take a step back and decline certain challenges, which was equally gratifying. The local authorities and the police were accustomed to such shenanigans. The highlight of our escapades was undoubtedly the flat crawls. But

The university years of experimentation and living my purpose

let us not digress. When you enrol in university, there is always ample room for enjoyment. Not only can you meet extraordinary individuals who become lifelong friends, but you also forge unforgettable bonds with those who are crucial to your journey during that phase of life. Among them were my dear friends Sandra, a Māori girl from Foxton, Manawatu, who eventually relocated to London to pursue a teaching career, and Kelly, a Māori girl from Rotorua, who coached our netball team. We always savoured the celebrations that followed our netball matches on Saturdays at the Royal Pub. This establishment served as the gathering spot for The Teachers College Netball Club and the Linton Army Rugby Club. Every girl adores the prospect of a complimentary beverage, especially when the Saturday night ritual of winning a $500 bar tab becomes a tradition. Our club needed to assemble a formidable group. We would rally the troops and ensure that five teams attended the pub. As students, we never fretted about drinks on Saturdays, as many of our teammates were non-drinkers. Sandra, Kelly, and I always contributed our fair share to maximize the bar tab.

Hazel at Christchurch Airport off to Lincoln University Garden Party

Hazel with Michelle at Lincoln University Garden Party

Hazel with Phillipa at the teacher's college graduation party

The university years of experimentation and living my purpose

Hazel with the girls getting ready to drink tequila shots

During my time as a member of the student executive at Massey University College of Education, I applied for an outdoor scholarship to participate in Outward Bound in Anikiwa, Picton. Outward Bound New Zealand is a non-profit organization that focuses on providing experiential education in the great outdoors. The primary aim of this program is to assist participants in realizing their full potential through various challenges in an outdoor setting. To cover the costs of the programme, I actively sought sponsorship from local Lions clubs and the Māori Women's Welfare League, which thankfully covered the remaining fees. In 1998, I embarked on my Outward-Bound adventure. I cannot emphasize enough how much I flourished in the *taio* (environment). The three-week programme presented the ultimate challenge for me, encompassing activities such as rock climbing, abseiling, sailing, tramping, and even sleeping in the snow. Surprisingly, these tasks came easily to me. However, my genuine challenge lay in supporting those who were less confident in outdoor activities. One memory that forever stays with me is the time I assisted Alice in navigating around the cutta, a large sailing boat, during a swimming exercise in freezing water. Alice, being nervous and showing anxiety needed some support to feel confident in swimming, even though she was provided with a life jacket for safety. Following my lap, I swam alongside Alice, speaking to her calmly and reassuringly providing encouragement throughout. This experience taught me the invaluable lesson of patience when working with others. In most scenarios, it is crucial to instil a sense of confidence and reassurance in people, reassuring them they will be all right. Although it required time and effort, witnessing Alice's immense relief and sense of accomplishment when she did not give up was truly rewarding.

The value of an Outward-Bound Experience

Before my 21st birthday, I was fortunate to go to Outward Bound. Outward Bound (OB) was founded by Kurt Hahn in England in 1941. Kurt was an educator and founded the Duke of Edinburgh's Award Scheme and the United World Colleges. The New Zealand Outward Bound Trust is a unique provider of traditional values and a focus on meeting the needs of people in New Zealand. The outdoor experiential course uses the outdoors and creative mediums to accelerate learning. The highly skilled instructors delivered a combination of these activities: sailing, kayaking, high ropes, rock climbing, solo experience, tramping, and physical training. One of the physically demanding attributes that is needed to have a great time at OB is to simply turn up. A positive aspect of OB is you do not need any outdoor experience to participate. The combination of physical, mental, and emotional challenges in a safe environment leads to honest reflection on personal values and goals. The benefits of doing an OB course for me included collaboratively working in a close team, also known as a watch which personally:

The university years of experimentation and living my purpose

- Increased my confidence and self-esteem.
- Improved my communication skills.
- Increased my ability to have a good relationship with others.
- Increased my accountability and wisdom to think.
- A balance in mind, body, and soul.

OB is in the Marlborough Sounds, South Island of New Zealand. OB is surrounded by beautiful coastlines, waterways, and bush. The classroom for OB would make anyone want to live there as the serene beauty of being one in nature, and the sound of the native birds captures a way of being.

Hazel with Hillary Watch at Outward Bound

Living life and experimentation in your twenties

Throughout my journey spanning over three years at university, I had the wonderful opportunity to meet a diverse range of individuals. As a university student, I was set in pursuing my passion and preparing myself to become a certified and licensed educator. At the end of each academic year, I would return to my hometown of Wairoa. During this time, I would work as a lifeguard at the local swimming pool, as well as taking up employment as a waitress and bar attendant at the Frazertown Tavern. Located approximately 10 kilometres outside of Wairoa, the Frazertown Tavern served as the gathering spot for many farmers and labourers who would unwind there after a long day's work. Interestingly, this establishment also was one of my father's preferred watering holes, where he would frequently meet up with his close friend Jacko, a fellow freezing worker based in the Beef House at Affco in Wairoa. During this period, I crossed paths with Paul and Marque, an exceptionally supportive couple deeply involved in the local Frazertown and Wairoa communities. Marque graciously offered me part-time employment for three consecutive years during my university breaks.

During my time at the tavern, I held the responsibility of being the designated driver, ensuring the safe transportation of both my father and Jacko. It was in this setting that I learned valuable lessons about playing pool. Jacko, a formidable individual known as the Red Devil within the Waiau Rugby Club, and my father, a steadfast member devoted to Tapuae Rugby Club and likened to a ninja turtle, imparted their knowledge upon me. It was truly an honour to meet my father's colleagues and socialize with his friends, as they held him in high regard at his workplace. On Friday evenings, while participating in their casual touch rugby team, I witnessed the actions and behaviours that these natural leaders employed to bring teams and people together. Their magnetic character and presence attracted others, thanks to the

The university years of experimentation and living my purpose

influential power they possessed, commonly referred to as '*mana*'. What set both Jacko and my father apart was their shared value of caring for others and treating everyone with respect. They followed the principles of the old ways, where honour and integrity held great significance in both personal and communal aspects of life. Through their actions, they showed the importance of fostering a strong sense of community.

Playing touch rugby provided immense enjoyment as it encompassed teamwork and fostered relationships, creating a sense of community among individuals. It did not matter if one possessed exceptional skills or not; what truly mattered was that everyone took a step forward and embraced the sport. Jacko played a crucial role in facilitating the integration of newcomers like me into this tight-knit community. During one match, I was substituted into play, and a teammate threw a remarkable pass that I caught from the opposite side of the field. I swiftly ran towards the try line and successfully scored. Interestingly, back then, girls were awarded double points for their tries. Despite winning the game, what truly struck me was the unwavering belief in the eyes of my fellow teammates as they witnessed my catch. Instead of correcting Jacko, who mistakenly believed my name to be Angel, I chose not to shatter the euphoria. Consequently, whenever we played touch rugby, Jacko would call me Angel, while the rest of the team would correct him, saying it is Hazel. The moral of this story lies in the understanding that we need not rectify every minor mistake others make. It implies relinquishing the need for constant control. Ultimately, I grew to adore my nickname as Angel, as both my dad and Jacko held me in high regard.

During my time at university, I had the extraordinary opportunity to encounter numerous exceptional individuals. As a natural progression, I shared accommodation with some close friends. In my second year, following Blair Tennant, I embarked on a flatting adventure with five girls from the hostel. What was supposed to be an exciting chapter turned into a harrowing ordeal with our first flat. Regrettably, our landlord insisted on a retainer fee for the holidays, which we duly paid in advance. However, upon returning to the flat, we discovered that other students had taken up residence in our rented space. It was an absolute disgrace, particularly considering that this landlord held a prominent position as the president of the landlord association in Palmerston North. At that moment, I felt a deep sense of responsibility to confront this individual. We pursued mediation at the Tenancy Tribunal, where the support officer demonstrated a lack of integrity and fairness. The memory of the despair in the girls' eyes and the anger on the faces of our fathers will forever be etched in my mind. My father was furious about the way we were mistreated. Because of this episode, we lost $300 from the $1500 retainer. To this day, we are uncertain for what the deduction was for. They were bloody crooks at the Tenancy Tribunal in Palmerston North. Despite this setback, we persevered on that same day with unwavering support from our crews and friends, and we secured another flat on the terrace, conveniently located near the hospital. Flatting with the girls was great fun and many memorable moments of revelry and friendships were made. Two of us needed to walk through each other's rooms, which posed a minor inconvenience when hosting guests. However, we made it work and adapted to the circumstances.

During my final year, my good friend Sandra, whom I used to play netball with, was searching for a flatmate. Since I was also in search of a place to stay, I gladly moved in to assist her. Sandra and I were inseparable and had a knack for embracing life to the fullest. We would party relentlessly, jamming to the tunes of Venga Boys, and engaging in all sorts of silly antics typical of university students. Sandra had recently started teaching in Levin, and as I was approaching the end of my studies, she opened doors for me by providing my first opportunity

The university years of experimentation and living my purpose

for relieving work. I understood accepting this opportunity was a smart move, as it would grant me valuable experience while I awaited my graduation. After some time, Sandra made the courageous decision to move to London, and she found me a place to live with her close friend, Debz. Debz was amazing; she made my last flatting experience in Palmerston North truly unforgettable. Our house was filled with countless enjoyable moments and cherished memories. However, as my studies ended, it was time for me to bid farewell to that chapter of my life and prepare to move to Wairoa. Sandra's actions highlighted her unwavering determination to forge ahead in life. By venturing to London, she took the risks one must face when confronted with hardships.

Hazel and Sandra before she headed off to London out tiki touring in Wairoa

Hazel and Sandra celebrating my graduation in the square at Palmerston North

The university years imparted valuable lessons to me, primarily emphasizing the importance of hard work. I completed my conjoint programme and realized that I needed to keep striving for my goal: becoming a certified registered teacher. This chapter teaches us the significance of dedication to learning and making plans once we achieve our objectives. I passionately believe that meticulous planning plays a pivotal role in achieving success. My journey highlights the necessity of self-development. Even in the face of adversity, we can move forward instead of backward, transforming failures into stepping stones. Through unwavering determination, we can accomplish anything we truly desire. Therefore, my story serves as a gentle reminder to all readers, whether their aspirations involve higher education or embarking on other significant endeavours. Our habits wield immense power, shaping our trajectory and laying the foundation for accomplishment. By embracing discipline, determination, and the support of a supportive community, we can surmount any obstacle

The university years of experimentation and living my purpose

Hazel's early years relief teaching in 1999 in local primary schools in Levin and rural Horowhenua

The university years imparted valuable lessons to me, primarily in our pursuit of greatness. And always remember, never shy away from daring dreams, for it is within those audacious aspirations that our true potential resides.

Hazel and Phillipa best buddies celebrating at Turitea main gate campus in Palmerston North

The university years of experimentation and living my purpose

Vic, Hazel and Dad celebrating in the square after graduation in Palmerston North

Angie, Rhonda and Hazel celebrating attending the after-ball graduation at the Palmerston North Arena

6 KEY TIPS FROM CHAPTER 4:

1. Dare to dream, take risks, and have new adventures.
2. Develop a champion mindset and surround yourself with good people. Celebrate your wins!
3. Apply yourself and maintain good habits and routines.
4. Live a little and keep balance.
5. Stand-up and never back down, even if you are doing it alone.
6. Get involved in a community and support others.

This chapter introduced the leadership and personal experiences of my university and early career years. Secondly, the chapter provides in-depth details of how authentic leadership was nurtured, how resilience is strengthened through different personal and professional experiences, and the importance of living one's purpose to have a fulfilling and rich life. The statement above reflects what is needed to develop authentic leadership. Here is the breakdown of the key elements:

1. *Authentic Leadership*:

- The concept of authentic leadership emphasises being genuine and true to oneself, and transparent in one's leadership approach.
- Authentic leaders are open about their values, beliefs, and experiences, fostering trust and connection with others.

2. ***Lived Experiences as Shapers of Character***:

    - The acknowledgment that lived experiences shape our character suggests that authenticity is deeply rooted in the unique journey of an individual.
    - Each experience contributes to the development of qualities and perspectives that define a leader's character.

3. ***Challenges as Stepping Stones:***

    - The metaphor of challenges as stepping stones implies a positive and growth-oriented mindset.
    - Authentic leaders view challenges not as obstacles but as opportunities for learning, development, and building resilience.

4. ***Reminding Us of Resilience:***

    - The statement reinforces the idea that resilience is a key quality in leadership.
    - Every challenge faced becomes a reminder that resilience is a necessary attribute for overcoming obstacles and adversities.

5. ***Continuous Journey of Becoming***:

    - The phrase 'stepping stone toward becoming' implies that authentic leadership is an ongoing journey.
    - Leadership is not a static state, but a continuous process of growth and development through experiences and challenges.

6. ***Transformative Nature of Challenges:***

- Challenges are not only hurdles, but transformative experiences.
- Overcoming challenges contributes to personal and professional growth, moulding individuals into resilient and authentic leaders.

7. ***Connection to Character and Leadership:***

- By emphasising the role of lived experiences in shaping character, the statement links authenticity directly to leadership.
- It suggests that an authentic leader's character is forged through the crucible of life's challenges.
- Authentic leadership is deeply intertwined with the lived experiences of an individual. Challenges, rather than being impediments, are integral to the journey, fostering resilience, and contributing to the development of an authentic leader's character.

> *Lived experience leadership is not about perfection; it is about embracing imperfections and using them as building blocks for authenticity and relatability.*

5

Transitioning from university to the workplace

The highlights of 1998

Two defining moments happened to me in 1998. I turned 21 years old without a baby and got my degree from Massey University College of Education. As part of my 21st birthday celebrations, Dad had a party at home. A group of my university friends came to Wairoa, we certainly had a great time. I was presented with Uncle Pat's 21st key, which sits on top of my drawer next to my bed. The glory of this twenty-first cup and the history associated with it speaks of his legacy to act with integrity and honour. Another time was when I felt my focus and devotion go astray and almost forced me to leave university. But after some talking and a glass of wine, my friend Jane was able to reaffirm to me it was okay, and that I was going to get through it. What matters is that I did not give up on my dreams. My dream was so much bigger than me and I wanted to finish my diploma but the pressure I put on myself, the internal dialogue that went on in my mind, almost made me drop out of university, and thank God, I kept pushing myself. I would not be where I am now.

Our self-imposed beliefs can affect our positivity. As I neared the completion of my studies, I struggled with the idea of planning for the future and obtaining a teacher's registration. Things may get messy around you, but believe me, it is part of the next stage in your journey. I had a tough time finding a teaching opportunity close to home in Wairoa.

Transitioning from university to the workplace

Dad presenting my 21st key and Uncle Pat's 21st cup presented to him on 15.09.1962

Uncle Pat with his best mate Arthur after playing a rugby game for Petone.

Hazel cutting her 21st birthday cake with mum and dad. The whānau from Te Teko in the front and my little sister Caroline to the side in Wairoa

Hukarere Māori Girls College

My motto in life is not to give up. I finally landed a job after placing over thirty applications. The difficulty some graduates face in finding a job after completing their qualifications is often disregarded by many universities. I gained my first job at Hukarere Māori Girls' College. I moved from Wairoa to Napier and lived in a couple of different places before landing with two brothers in a flat on Hastings Street in Napier. It was your typical boys' house, with the lads having a few drinks and leaving the key in the door. The normal antics you get with country boys and the house drinks they would have with their friends.

My time at Hukarere was exceedingly difficult. I had a head teacher bullying and being dismissive towards me. I was fortunate to have two excellent senior teachers from the PPTA union to help me navigate such emotional turmoil. The school was extremely poor. The buildings were in a state of disrepair. It was interesting to see how education could be so different at a smaller school than what I was used to when teaching in city schools in Palmerston North. The school was classified as decile 1a. The decile rating system used in mainstream schools in New Zealand was rather old and stratified according to the socioeconomic status of the community. Smaller school populations and lower decile numbers correspond to higher essential needs within the school community. My good friend Rhonda, her father owned the local burger Wisconsin joint in Napier. We were senior students together at Massey and spent many good nights at Palmerston North as well as in Napier. I was playing netball at a local sports club, but I needed to chase my itch to get my teachers' registration. I knew I had to leave Hukarere.

My adventures to Te Teko

I needed a change from Hukarere and went to Te Teko after spending a night with my cousins in Ohope. Through a night out with the cousins, I made a friend who introduced me to Noel. I landed my first full-time job teaching at Putauaki Primary School for a term. Life was great, and us teachers had a lot of fun together. We used to socialize on Fridays for drinks, which was a great way to bond. Although my job was not permanent, I enjoyed working at Putauaki and wanted to secure a full-time position. I was living in an outside shed flat with Sammy at my mum's house, and we used to have some great garage parties. I met some amazing people who helped me to understand myself better and taught me what I wanted in a relationship. I eventually found another teaching job at Te Mahoe Primary School and formed a great connection with Jenny and Adele. Jenny helped me with mentoring to get my teacher's registration started, which was crucial to being able to work in New Zealand schools. The challenge I faced was finding a permanent full-time teaching role. I was willing to do any job anywhere in New Zealand, but the education system is such that it is up to the graduate to find a school to get registered. I was determined to get the registration, and Jenny and I planned it together. After securing a permanent position at Waiariki Institute of Technology, I met another great group of friends. We used to hang out together and have Friday afternoon social drinks at Whakatane High and later go out to the Boiler room, the Comm, and Marist Clubrooms in Whakatane. These were some of the best times I had with work colleagues. The Christmas parties were fairly good too, as we went to the Rugby clubrooms in Paeroa and Poroporo and out to Ohope Beach.

Hazel and Aunty Rihi celebrating Xmas at a work function in Tauranga Harbour

Transitioning from university to the workplace

Hazel and work friends celebrating our Xmas work function on a Mystery Bus Tour in Whakatane. First stop at Whakatane Marist and then Poroporo Rugby Sports Clubroom

Waiariki Institute of Technology, Whakatane

While at Waiariki Institute of Technology, I experienced many challenging leadership events. I believe I failed miserably in the role. So many institutional structures were making it difficult to succeed. The head office in Rotorua was upset with the amount of funding that the pilot programme was getting. The women in charge of Rotorua in the other satellite course had a demeaning way towards me and were never helpful. It was a struggle to get resources and help from them. So, with the help of Jenny and other external supporters, I battled on for two years. I was not closer to my goal of teacher registration, and I knew I needed to get back into a school. I left Waiariki after a total blowout.

Exhausted from the internal pressure of a role and dealing with unhelpful collaborators. I floated in between schools for the last part of November doing relieving in Wairoa. This gave me a bit of semblance of order. I was in a relationship at the time and unsure of where it would lead, I headed to Australia as part of my Overseas Experience (OE), however, I never made it to London because I still did not have my teacher's registration and thought I would give it a shot with my then boyfriend. In 2003, my next move was to Cambridge and later Hamilton. I moved in with my boyfriend, but after six months together, the relationship ended; time to call it quits. It was the best call I had made that led up to the demise of the relationship. A series of events took place, and I learned from that failed relationship to never be someone's option. See you must be in tune with your intuition. You will see obvious signs that are red flags when your partner is being dodgy and acting suspiciously. For example, your partner will provide excuses for why they have not returned home and use other people as a backup to explain their behaviour. It was obvious when I look back at my life that I was growing and needed more in my life, and we were both moving in different directions. Sometimes love can be so blind that you are oblivious to what is around you and in challenging moments you learn the character of a person, the integrity they have, and their intentions for you.

As a result, and having the power to make such an important decision, I had a couple of work colleagues come and help me pack my stuff and leave the flat in Cambridge. It was a necessary move for me. I finally was now back on track, chasing my itch. I was working at a Māori tertiary training provider where I experienced a stormy affair of challenges. I felt I had miserably failed in my roles and was confronted with workplace bullying. The redeeming feature was I found a lovely bunch of *wahine toa* who I naturally gravitated towards. Being with Māori women reminded me of the times I had with the nannies of the Otaki Tararua Branch of the Māori Women's Welfare League. I also met another *kaumātua* (elder), Jim who was so warm and kind towards me and helped me through the employment mediation process. With the support of my family, Dad and Caroline helped me through leaving Hamilton and I took time out in Wairoa to reset before I engaged in the employment mediation process. A plus side from my experience in Hamilton was I finally got my teacher's registration; it took four years to get it post-graduation. But reaming with joy, I knew I was on my way to better pastures.

Crisis in the workplace - Tips for dealing with employment mediation

Sometimes in the workplace, you can find yourself in serious trouble. I must agree it is never easy when someone is alleging that you have done wrongdoing to students. It hurts your soul and can destroy your confidence and impact on your wellbeing. Sometimes, it is impossible to avoid such events and you need to embrace this as a path to further learning and growth as an individual. Nobody talks about these types of situations and being quite young at the time (26 years old), it was my first hard challenge of standing up to authority. An employment problem is where the employer identifies an employee has done something wrong.

Several big changes were happening in tertiary education in New Zealand with the introduction of alternative Māori educational establishments with the status of *Wānanga* (place of learning). The place I worked at was an alternative place for Māori to study higher education programmes. I had my *kaumātua* from Te Teko guiding me along and my family to deal with the organisational dilemma I was facing.

An organisational dilemma is defined as an issue between organisational benefits versus individual member's welfare. Structural dilemmas concern dilemmas faced by groups or individuals because of structural relationships.

If you are ever faced with a warning, formal warning by written notice, and called to a disciplinary meeting, it is important you keep the faith. Understand that procedural process must be followed, and often not, sometimes the employer, may not be following due process because they lack the nuance and integrity to care for the employee and are downright acting like a bully. You must own the situation and stand firm on your principles. I never back down from a fight or a call of challenge. I was no quitter. I had worked too hard to allow the organisation I was working at affect my teacher's registration.

Always have a support person when you go into such meetings. Being called into an office is difficult, having management tell you inaccuracies of your performance is not fair, even more so if they are not acting according to *tikanga Māori* (cultural practices and protocols) that are aligned with the Māori values of *tika* (being correct) and *pono* (genuine). I spent a lot of time on the phone with my *kaumātua* in Te Teko, talking over how I was going to get through the situation. My *kaumātua* advice was to keep pushing forward and go start that, Masters. I did not have any inclination to do Masters. I could not see what was ahead of me. I felt I was drowning and needed help. My family came to the rescue and my Dad told me to come home and have a rest in Wairoa.

Here I faced dealing with a very high-level situation. I was getting disciplined as well as being made redundant. Dealing with this new challenge was a difficult process. I certainly learnt a lot about myself. I had engaged in the union, but they were not helpful. I then engaged the help of an employment lawyer. Well, that lawyer did not really help me, he just extended the situation, and he should have requested Employment Mediation Services. Some months had passed, and I finally got another letter that requested I attend. It was by a whim of driving around and walking into a couple of offices in Hamilton that I finally found the right lawyer for me. Kate was amazing. She was highly efficient and sorted the issue out for me at the first meeting. By the end of our initial meeting, she had a clear plan to resolve the issue, and a date in mediation services. Employment Mediation Services, have the parties sit in the room and they control the meeting. Kate got the result I needed an apology and a settlement. I would like to say that was one of the hardest times in my life. I think looking at where I am today, it was only preparing me for what was to come.

Sometimes, you find yourself navigating unfound territories in your workplace. It is the time you spend with trusted support networks that can help you avoid the overload and mental and emotional angst that come from engaging in workplace issues. Another critical step is to be aware of the body's reaction to stress. Stress can be seen in many ways within the body. Listen to the warning signs that are internally going off inside of you. Our bodies are intricate vessels that tell us when things are not right. Your body can act in peculiar ways, such as experiencing a lack of sleep, a decrease in appetite, a sense of constant worry, bloating, and weight gain. The following points that I list are a summary of what you can do to deal with challenging workplace issues:

1. Make sure before any employment matter happens, sign the collective and know your rights.
2. Calm down and breathe. Getting a letter is difficult when you are asked to attend a disciplinary meeting. Ask for an agenda for the meeting and take a support person.
3. Speak to the union delegate or if you can engage the services of an employment lawyer. Be mindful that lawyers are not cheap and watch out for lawyers who like talking and give no clear direction as to how they are going to solve your issue. A good lawyer will make the trouble go away. They will ensure you are served well and are highly planned and advise you on the steps to solving the issue.
4. Prepare before you go to the first meeting. Have a strategy for answering difficult questions. Often, I like to have a paper and pen and the letter they sent you in front of me.
5. While the Human Resource (HR) advisor or the employer's representative, is talking, just listen to their points. Avoid responding, wait to hear what they have to say. It is extremely easy to get into an intense argument. If necessary, note this down on the notepad. Still, do this if you have the union delegate or lawyer with you.
6. Always remain calm under pressure. Take the time to clarify each point raised by the employer's representative, and if necessary, ask for clarification of any points of reference. Watch the body language of the speaker. It is a clear giveaway; if they are attacking you. In any situation, it is their role to make sure that the meeting is being conducted in a safe environment.

7. You may have to watch out for patronising interrogation methods. Employer's representatives will do anything to make it seem like you are in the wrong. You will always feel nervous and worried because it is an unfamiliar experience. All I can say, is if you have done nothing wrong, stand firm. In all instances, do not let people *takahi o taku mana* (stamp on your prestige).
8. Take a lawyer and let them do all the talking. It is your lawyer's role to know the law and ensure you get a fair deal.

What this chapter shows you is life can be hard and rewarding. Sometimes life throws you challenges. It is in these moments your character is tested and your power to make informed decisions can either lead you to success or failure. In these trying times, having the faith that everything will be all right is vitally important to chasing your itch. What I can say is that from my experience you only become stronger when tough times happen, and your *tupuna* (elders) are guiding you to fulfilling your purpose in life. The support network I had during these different stages of establishing my professional career helped me to become better in my ability to navigate organisational dilemmas and spot the red flags in educational organisations and people. Often the difficulty, as a Māori woman navigating the leadership space is you will find many green eyed monsters who will be jealous of who you are and will see the gifts that you may not consciously be aware of. Leading with purpose from my perspective is about being true to yourself and bringing people along on the journey of transformational change. The difficulty of being true to yourself is that you often will learn the hard way and get knocked down, as part of, building your emotional intelligence and being prepared for a greater purpose in your future.

6 KEY TIPS FROM CHAPTER 5:

1. Recharge, reflect, and reset your internal compass. Understand that reaching your potential does not happen overnight.
2. Be selective about relationships. Choose wisely who spends time with you.
3. Focus on endurance. It takes time to become successful.
4. Be generous to yourself, invest in learning and new experiences.
5. Aim to be your personal best every day.
6. Share your knowledge with others.

This chapter captures aspects of lived experience and how learning can be interpreted from my narratives of transitioning from the university years to the workplace. Here is the breakdown of the key elements within the statement for developing ideals for leadership as an authentic leader:

1. ***Lived Experience Leadership***:

- This style of leadership is informed and shaped by one's personal experiences, emphasising that authenticity comes from real-life encounters.

2. ***Not About Perfection***:

- The rejection of perfectionism suggests an understanding that leaders are human and inherently flawed.

- It challenges the notion that leadership requires flawless execution and highlights the importance of embracing imperfections.

3. *Embracing Imperfections*:

    - The heart of the statement lies in the acceptance and acknowledgment of imperfections.
    - Embracing imperfections signifies a willingness to be vulnerable and genuine in leadership roles.

4. *Building Blocks for Authenticity*:

    - Imperfections are not seen as weaknesses but as essential components that contribute to authenticity.
    - Authenticity in leadership involves being true to oneself, and imperfections are part of that truth.

5. *Building Blocks for Relatability*:

    - The idea that imperfections serve as building blocks implies that they are not hindrances but foundational elements.
    - Imperfections become relatable aspects that connect leaders with others on a human level.

6. *Emphasis on Authenticity and Relatability*:

    - The statement places a high value on authenticity and relatability in leadership.
    - Authentic leaders are genuine, and relatability fosters stronger connections with those they lead.

7. ***Humanizing Leadership***:

- By rejecting perfection and embracing imperfections, the statement humanizes leadership.
- It communicates that leaders are not untouchable figures but individuals with their own strengths and weaknesses.

8. ***Encouraging a Positive Leadership Culture***:

- Embracing imperfections creates a culture where mistakes are not feared but seen as opportunities for growth.
- It encourages a positive approach to leadership development and continuous improvement.

In summary, the essence of lived experience leadership implies that 'being real' is true leadership and not about presenting a facade of perfection, but rather it is okay to embrace imperfections. From my lens, embracing imperfection encourages leaders to use these imperfections as foundational elements for authenticity and relatability, fostering a positive and genuine leadership culture.

> True leadership emerges when we find the strength to share our personal narratives, transforming vulnerabilities into beacons of inspiration for others.

6

Transitioning from Te Kauwhata to Auckland

[Re] setting and [Re] energising and evolving my true purpose

So, after the rough time I had experienced from my last workplace, it was time to get back up on my feet and bounce back to myself. I started reviewing jobs in the Education Gazette and saw a position that fit with what I was looking for. The advertisement was appealing as it came with an opportunity to live in a teacher's house. I applied for the teaching vacancy at Te Kauwhata College, where I could teach physical education and maths for six hours a week. One reason for choosing this position was I saw it as an opportunity to start fresh, learn from my past experiences, and take on new challenges.

Te Kauwhata is a small rural community south of Hamilton and is about fifteen minutes from Pukekohe, and is very close to Bombay Hills. I had a strong desire to move into a permanent leadership position, and I was already thinking about the possibility of becoming a department head and eventually a principal. At my interview, I met the principal, Colin. I took an instant liking to Colin, whom I considered to be a well-astute leader, who took me under his wing and helped me to progress into middle management and leadership at the school. At the interview, Colin asked me some direct questions, which I answered with honesty and integrity. During this interview I had nothing to lose as I knew the school needed a teacher asap. I also needed a place to live and reset myself. In interviews, you generally have an idea of how things are going to evolve. I felt I had a good chance of getting the job. I also knew that if I took the position, it would set me up for the permanent position that was being advertised for the following year.

I stayed for two and half years and loved teaching physical education and living in the countryside. Living in Te Kauwhata reminded me of being in Wairoa. The location of the school was close to other rural towns like Thames and Coromandel and was within driving distance to Hamilton City. I always kept myself active while living in Te Kauwhata. I got involved in the community, started playing golf, joined the gym in Hamilton, and played winter hockey in Ngatea. Being a small school, it was easy to make friends with the other teachers. There was a good mix of both young and more mature teachers. I made some great teaching friends while I was at the College.

I enjoyed collaborating with my team Julie, Quentin, and Kerry, who made my time at the school memorable. Kerry was my Head of Department (HOD) and had completed his training in Wales. He had left Wales and came straight to the Te Kauwhata College as a young teacher. Julie had also spent most of her time at the school and her husband Terry also worked in a relieving capacity too. I met Vai, Gillian, Geneive, and Rosie. They had been teaching at the school for some time. We made a great community between us all. Great women banding together and enjoying our time together. I already met Rosie when I worked at Waiariki in Whakatane. Rosie was to become a close friend who supported me in my principal's position when I made the move up to the Far North. As the new teacher on the block. I had many invites to each of the girl's homes. We celebrated my 30th in style down at the farm and the local pub, which went over three days. The milestones you make are worth celebrating and reminiscing on the growth that you have made in life.

What I liked about Te Kauwhata College was my principal shared common values of *mana*, integrity, and service. Colin was a man of principles who had a great heart to do well for Māori. His encouragement and mentoring of me into management roles landed my first leadership unit at the college and then later my promotion to Head of Department in Auckland. Colin was incredibly supportive of Māori initiatives and particularly, supporting the building of the *papakainga* complex. One of my joys with being at Te Kauwhata was my involvement with the Māori community in supporting the fundraising of the school *papakainga*.

A *papakainga* in schools was a mechanism to help schools like Te Kauwhata College build and strengthen their relationship with *whānau* and allow Māori students to strengthen their connection to their cultural identity as Māori. Girlie was an avid driver of the project, alongside the Māori school community. Girlie's approach to Māori things was *tūturu* (authentic). Her style of leadership was let us make it happen. Both Girlie and I were a great team. I did not know about golf, so I got a plan together with the Waikato Golf Association representative. I had written a sponsorship proposal, and Girlie and I set off together to speak with the local businesses in Te Kauwhata and Huntly to sponsor the school. What I can say is that the Charity Golf Tournament was a great event. The community was behind us, and we raised over $3000 after expenses. This profit went towards the *papakainga*.

I met my former partner in November 2007. After spending a couple of months dating each other, it felt like a good time to see where our chapter would lead to and give the relationship a go. I started looking at the next step in my career and ended up moving to Auckland in April 2008. Colin, my principal, gave me his blessings and the girls that I met wished me well on the journey ahead. I secured the head of department job at Marist College in Auckland. I made the move to Auckland and never looked back.

6 KEY TIPS FROM CHAPTER 6:

1. Life is too short. Take a leap of faith and jump.
2. Risks are necessary, act and be brave.
3. If you want something, drive towards it, not away from it.
4. Always reset the goal and aim for the next big dream.
5. Be true to yourself.
6. Try things. If it does not work, it is all right.

This chapter captures aspects of lived experience and the different aspects of leadership needed in personal relationships. Here is the breakdown of the key elements within the statement that revolves around authenticity, vulnerability, and inspiration:

1. ***True Leadership***:

    - The term 'true leadership' suggests a leadership that goes beyond superficial or traditional definitions.
    - It implies a deeper, more authentic expression of leadership.

2. ***Finding Strength in Sharing Personal Narratives***:

    - The acknowledgment that true leadership involves finding strength in sharing personal narratives highlights the courage required to be vulnerable and open.
    - Leaders are encouraged to draw strength from their own stories.

3. *Transforming Vulnerabilities*:

- The transformative aspect suggests vulnerabilities are not weaknesses, but opportunities for growth and empowerment.
- Leaders are called to turn vulnerabilities into sources of strength.

4. *Beacons of Inspiration*:

- The metaphor of "beacons of inspiration" conveys the idea that sharing personal narratives can serve as guiding lights for others.
- Leaders become sources of inspiration by being authentic and transparent about their experiences.

5. *Empowering Others through Personal Stories*:

- True leadership involves empowering others by sharing personal stories.
- It creates a sense of connection and relatability, inspiring others to overcome their challenges.

6. *Encouraging Openness and Transparency*:

- The statement encourages a leadership style that is open and transparent.
- It suggests that leaders who share personal narratives foster a culture of trust and authenticity within their teams.

7. ***Building Trust and Connection***:

- By sharing personal narratives, leaders build trust with those they lead.
- It creates a sense of connection and understanding, strengthening the leader-follower relationship.

8. ***Inspiring Through Authenticity:***

- The crux of the statement is that true leadership inspires through authenticity.
- Leaders who are genuine and open about their own experiences can have a profound impact on those around them.
- In summary, the statement at the beginning of the chapter articulates that true leadership involves embracing vulnerability by finding strength in sharing personal narratives. By transforming vulnerabilities into beacons of inspiration, leaders create a powerful and authentic impact, fostering trust, connection, and inspiration among those they lead.

> *In the journey of lived experience, each setback is a lesson, each triumph a testament to the power of perseverance and self-discovery.*

7

Courage to grow and invest time on personal relationships and career advancement

Creating space and time for personal relationships and professional growth

If you meet someone who gives you those warm fuzzy feelings inside and makes you wonder if there is a genuine connection. From my lens it is an easy decision. You have made a connection and if you are ready to let someone into your world and your space, then it's time to open and bring those walls or barriers down. Daring to take a risk, and stepping forward is not easy if you have been burnt before in relationships, I think it is worth taking the time to get to know people you are interested in and see how they can complement and bring value to your life.

The move from Te Kauwhata to Auckland was simple. I ran with my heart and head towards my dream of becoming a leader in my field and towards building the connection with my future partner. Managing your love life and career involves a balancing act. It is possible, but it requires a bit of hard work, and dedication. It is natural to feel challenged by balancing your career and working towards being the best partner. On some days, it can be incredibly stressful, which makes you question if the relationship may last. The truth of the matter is that both parties must put the hard work and effort into making the relationship work.

Opportunities are always there for the taking. I feel that there are two ways that opportunities present. You either are in the place at the right time or you go out and make an opportunity for yourself. I had just entered the beginning of a long-term relationship that coincided with my dream of becoming a principal. The growth I was working through was advancing my educational leadership career alongside balancing this with my love life.

For the both of us to give the relationship a good crack, it made sense for me to move to Auckland. Hence, I started looking for teaching management positions in Auckland. In my teaching career, I had always been in the lowest decile schools with a high proportion of Māori students or working in predominantly Māori communities. I had three interviews for middle management positions that had a focus on health and physical education. The school I eventually ended up at was Marist College, an integrated Catholic girl's secondary high school in Mount Albert, Auckland. The school catered for girls from year 7 through to year 13 with an education founded on the Catholic faith.

I had made my way to Auckland. Auckland was fascinating. It was different from the slower, more peaceful way of Te Kauwhata. Moving from a half-acre home into a small 56-square-metre apartment, 15 storeys high was a different experience for me. It did not matter to me because it was an adventure. It did not take long for Auckland to grow on me. With so many restaurants, pubs, and things to do, I enjoyed the city. It was even better because I was sharing the time with my best friend. Living in Zest Apartments was close to everything in downtown Auckland. I had to downsize and give most of the stuff I had away before moving into the little apartment.

What I would say was that my good friend Olivia reminded me of my friends that I had in Te Kauwhata. She was a lifesaver when it came to moving. In hindsight, when it was time to move, I should have put my foot down and insisted my former partner help with the moving of our home. I guess sometimes, we try to compromise and keep the peace. Looking back at this moment, it was a red flag, as the same issue was to reappear in the next move from Freemans Bay to Papatoetoe. Oh, such learning curves that either make or break you. But knowing the person I was, I kept charging ahead to get the task completed because the work needed to be done.

The learning I gained from being in the head of department role at Marist revealed to me it was time to keep moving ahead to becoming a principal. I missed being with Māori students and decided to resign from my job before my wedding. I felt that it was the best move for my career. In most situations, you often will have an intrinsic feeling that is calling to you, some would say a calling from your *tupuna*. The staff at school were great. They put on a bridal shower for me and I was getting ready to go to Rarotonga for our wedding. It was the first time for both families to be meeting. I fell in love with Rarotonga, the freedom and the culture that the island's life brings.

The Rarotongan wedding with *whānau*

Courage to grow and invest time

On my return home, I finished the last months off at Marist and secured a role at Manurewa Intermediate in South Auckland. I will always be grateful for the experiences of being introduced to a new country and visiting new places like Scotland and Ireland. International travel opens your eyes. You feel more appreciative of the privilege you have with your own country. To finish the year off, I took my first trip to London. Some ten years prior, I was supposed to go to London for my Overseas Exchange (OE) but it just didn't happen. It felt like I had ticked off a dream of mine. We went to America, and another dream was ticked off the list. We went to Disneyland, and it is what they say - magical.

The difference between Mt Albert and Manurewa was huge. Mt Albert was a richer community and there was a presence of elitism. Manurewa felt like home and I was back working with Māori students and it was during this time I started my Masters journey. I was encouraged earlier by my *kaumātua* and by my principal Iain. Iain was the type of leader who was visionary. He made things happen, and if you weren't prepared to go the extra mile, step aside and keep moving on. I loved returning to postgraduate studies and fell back into my pattern of chasing the itch. During my time, I made some great friends at Manurewa. Bev was my girl. She was a Cook Islander and had the best singing voice on her. Watch out, Alicia Keys. Rachel, Bev, Ruth, and I had some great nights out on the town, and we were inseparable.

While at Manurewa Intermediate, the principal asked if I could help Paula. I said, of course. From the moment we met, we were best mates. Miss Paula Shea was my angel in disguise who knew how to party and was one of the most amazing friends I had made while teaching at Manurewa Intermediate. Paula lived on K Road, known as Karangahape Road. She was the life of the party who never turned people away and would give the shirt off her back. I loved Paula because she was wise and had so much intergenerational knowledge of teaching and working in remote communities. I had met Paula earlier in my career during an interview in Mangakino. In 2003 I went for the interview at Mangakino Area School where Paula was the Deputy Principal. I was prepared to do almost anything to get my teacher's registration. Mangakino is a small town that sits on the banks of the Waikato River behind Taupo. I stayed with Paula that night. We went down to the local pub and had a great yarn. Well, the next day at the interview, I was told the role was mine, but it wasn't to be as I was not prepared to move to such an isolated community. After reconnecting at Manurewa, who would know that I would take on a similar role but as Principal in an isolated community.

I had a great two years at Manurewa Intermediate. I saw one way how an effective school can make a difference for all students, particularly for Pacific and Māori students. But I wanted to step up and become a Principal. So off I applied for three leadership roles. I did one interview and got the role at Herekino. Now Herekino is a remote rural community in the upper part of Northland. So big decisions were made, and my husband did not want to move with me to the area. He stayed behind in Auckland and we had a long-term relationship away from each other for two years. I would have to say that this was one of the hardest decisions I had to make, give up on my dream, and stay or go. So I went, and we made it work.

I was fortunate that at the time I moved up north, my good friend Rosie had married a local honey farmer in Kohukohu. I spent the first nine months with them before finding an amazing apartment in Ahipara. I loved the amazing coastal beaches and the rustic life of the country, but I also missed being with my partner and living in Auckland. In those moments, I shifted my attention to my studies and committed to completing my postgraduate diploma. I had to think of the bigger picture, that it was all for a greater course. I was chasing my dream of completing my masters.

Being a school principal was an honour. I had worked diligently toward my dream, and it meant that my true purpose in life was about to evolve again. As a principal, I could make an impact and bring significant change to Māori students in their education. The role was not easy, and I struggled with the endless hours of administration and solving problems. I was working towards a scholarship that would allow me to complete my masters back in Auckland. My time in Herekino was rather short, two years, but invaluable. My time at the school was the impetus for my master's thesis research project. I wanted to explore and examine the impact of leadership in small rural primary schools and the challenges teaching principals face. I won the scholarship that allowed me 34 weeks off work and returned to Auckland.

Coming home to Auckland was a relief, and we celebrated with an amazing chef's dinner in the Viaduct. I was chasing my next step, completing my Masters of Educational Leadership and Management. Having a year away from work not only made a difference for my mind, soul, and body, it also meant I could also work on my marriage at a closer distance rather than across the other side of New Zealand. We could have a lot of fun and do new things together. I will always be grateful for the trips we took during my study leave. I got to see amazing places and visiting Dubai was another tick off my dream list. But it was time to reassess what I was going to do next. I was drained from being a principal and felt that there was more to life. I resigned from my role and fell into my next step, which was chasing my next itch, embarking on the doctoral journey.

Hazel on her Masters Graduation Day in 2015 wearing the Ngā Maihi hapū korowai at Aotea Town Square in Auckland

Courage to grow and invest time

Hazel at Māori Graduation Day in 2015 wearing the Ngā Maihi hapū korowai at Unitec in Mt Albert, Auckland

Some useful tips I learned along the way for managing a relationship alongside building your career may help you find more peace from within and stability:

1. ***Have emotional check ins – check your batteries***

    It is worthwhile to talk to see how your partner or friend/s are doing in person. Sometimes work can be so hectic that life can happen so fast. Remember not to let work overwhelm you and share the challenges that you have with your partner (or friend/s), no matter how horrific it is. Ask your partner (or friend/s) how they are feeling regularly. Do they feel heard and listened to or supported by you? Talk about what you both could do to feel more connected as part of building *whanaungatanga* (building relationships). In my situation, creativity had to come into play because of our opposing work times. Nothing is impossible if you put the time and effort into your relationships.

2. Send your partner a quick message via social media

There are many apps to use like Facebook Messenger or WhatsApp. It is great to let your partner know that you are thinking of them. Leave them an emoji or a special note.

3. Cement quality time – commit and invest in date times

Sometimes more than often, it is each person's responsibility to create space and dedicate time to the connection within the relationship. I think you work through that with your person, for me at least once a week is a great start depending on your commitment to work through prioritising your needs related to the partnership and the running of your house. It gives you both something to look forward to no matter how hectic work and your career looks like. If your time is limited, make your time count with your partner. There is no need for one of you to be chasing the other person to invest time and explain the relevance of cementing time together.

4. Turn on your ears – practice active listening

Become a better listener by being present because it will help your relationships. Here, you must discern the difference between hearing and listening. These are two different actions. Be mindful not to be looking at your phone or holding something in your hand that distracts from the conversation. Some useful tips after having a conversation are restating and summarising what your partner has shared with you in a couple of sentences. Give them a few non-verbal actions like looking at them directly, nodding your head when they are speaking and providing short verbal responses such as wow, I see, what then. To make someone feel heard, think of yourself as a mirror. Reflect to them that what you heard was important and that you seriously have heard them. For example, "I can see that what happened at work was important to you." Ask for their permission to give feedback and solutions on how your partner (or friend/s) may navigate the challenge. Say something like, "May I offer you some feedback?" They will either say yes or no. If they say no, respond by thanking them for their honesty and move on.

5. *Understand how to build your emotional intelligence*

Understand how emotions can impact living a more meaningful life with intention. When you are listening to the person who is speaking, see if you can suss out what the underlying emotion is that is affecting them. Are they feeling love, shame, anger, happiness, sadness, grief? Being able to recognise and navigate one's emotions is important to not let them boil over time and make situations worse between each other. There are many different emotion wheels that you can look at that can teach you how to build emotional intelligence. Understanding your own emotions and the emotions of others helps build *Whanaungatanga* (building relationships) within your relationships and get through challenges and complex situations.

6. *Establish healthy boundaries*

Creating healthy boundaries with yourself, others, and in the relationship itself is crucial. This involves establishing guidelines or *tikanga* (processes and practices) that both parties find acceptable and are expected to adhere to in the relationship. Having healthy boundaries for oneself is necessary as it teaches the other person what you feel is acceptable behaviour.

It's important to call out inappropriate behaviour. Never settle for people who talk down to you. Upon reflection, there were so many red flags that could have been addressed earlier. Going forward, I have learnt it is important to set and (re) set your boundaries at the beginning and during a relationship and approach this *kōrero* (talk) with gentleness. You do not want to spend all your time teaching someone how to treat you. It is important to never tolerate disrespect from anyone and to call them out on it. Sometimes it is necessary to leave the relationship for your *hauora*. *Hauora* captures the wholeness of a person from a Māori lens. *Hauora* encapsulates four dimensions that are interrelated and interconnected. It is like a house, where you need four pillars to have the house stand up. The house in its later stage refers to you, the individual. The four dimensions are *taha whānau* (social wellbeing – the connectedness you have with people and environment), *taha tinana* (physical wellbeing – having the ability to maintain a healthy quality of life to do daily activities without physical fatigue and stress), *taha hinengaro* (mental wellbeing – a person's thoughts, feelings, mind & conscience), and *taha wairua* (spiritual wellbeing – explores your relationship with the environment, people, and heritage in the past, present, and future.

7. **Dream together**

When you set time aside once a week (month), it is important to dream together and set goals. Make a list of the things you would like to do, and your other significant half may like to do.

8. *Reach out for help*

Do not keep things locked inside your head. I have always learnt to ask for help no matter what the situation is. Asking for help allows your other significant half to feel that they can do something for you. Never feel helpless in any situation. Two minds are better than one mind. And a problem shared is a problem halved.

9. *Love each other*

Always tell your partner I love you and I am here for you. Be available and make space for them no matter what is going on in your life. Give compliments and practice gratitude for what you have, because once it is gone, it is gone forever. Gifts are unnecessary; it is the little touches of praise and motivational uplifting that make the difference. Saying something like "I'm so proud of you" will surely touch your significant's heart.

6 KEY TIPS FROM CHAPTER 7:

1. Learn to take time out to relax from stressful situations.
2. *Whānau* are your greatest support systems. Reach out and ask for help.
3. Never be afraid to take a step back to reflect.
4. It's alright to change direction.
5. Listen to your gut. When it's time to move, do it.
6. Know that everything works out the way it is meant to.

This chapter captures the journey of my life in growing from personal relationships and progressing my career. Here is the breakdown of the key elements within the statement that revolves around the transformative nature of setbacks and triumphs. Let's break down the key elements:

1. ***Journey of Lived Experience***:

- The term 'journey' implies an ongoing and dynamic process, suggesting that life is a continuous and evolving series of experiences.

2. ***Setback as a Lesson***:

- Viewing setbacks as lessons implies a growth mindset.
- Each challenge becomes an opportunity for learning, resilience, and personal development.

3. ***Triumph as a Testament to Perseverance***:

    - Describing triumphs as a testament to perseverance highlights the enduring power of persistence and determination.
    - Success is not just an outcome but a reflection of the commitment to overcoming challenges.

4. ***Power of Perseverance***:

    - The emphasis on perseverance underscores its transformative power.
    - Perseverance is not only about enduring challenges but about growing stronger through the process.

5. ***Self-Discovery***:

    - The notion that each triumph is a testament to self-discovery suggests that success is not just external but contributes to a deeper understanding of oneself.
    - Success becomes a mirror reflecting one's strengths, values, and capabilities.

6. ***Continuous Learning and Growth***:

    - The idea that setbacks are lessons and triumphs are testaments reinforces the concept of continuous learning and growth.
    - Life's experiences, whether positive or negative, contribute to an individual's ongoing development.

7. ***Holistic Approach to Life***:

- The statement implies a holistic perspective on life, acknowledging that both setbacks and triumphs are integral parts of the human experience.
- It suggests that a well-lived life involves learning from challenges and celebrating successes.

8. ***Personal Resilience and Strength:***

- The power of perseverance and self-discovery reflects personal resilience and an inner strength that propels individuals forward in their journey.
- It implies an ability to navigate the complexities of life with resilience and adaptability.

In summary, acknowledge the importance of learning from setbacks, celebrating triumphs, and recognising the power of perseverance and self-discovery in shaping your ongoing personal growth and development.

> *Leading authentically requires the courage to navigate uncharted territories within ourselves, using the compass of our lived experiences to guide the way.*

8

Daring to be brave to chase a PhD and home ownership

Being brave and embracing the PhD journey

For some time after the principalship up north, I was searching for my next move. I had just finished my masters and was completing my pre-doctoral internship at Unitec in Auckland. I spent a good ten weeks collaborating with my supervisors. Dr Josie was the Head of *Māturanga Māori* at Unitec. She left a huge impact on me and guided me through the process of undertaking Kaupapa Māori research. I instinctively knew that doing the pre-doctoral internship was the right pathway for me. I enjoyed and loved working in the Kaupapa Māori space as it felt like home. After successfully completing the internship in 2016, I put in the PGR2 entry application for the doctoral programme and was successful. The internship gave me a couple of months of pay to cover the basics of our joint bills, but I could not contribute towards the joint savings. When you do a master's programme, it is exceedingly difficult to go back into a teacher's role. I realised I needed to do something different. I was over teaching in mainstream education, having to deal with the dilemmas of people who were not open minded and after 23 years of teaching, I became dissatisfied with the way New Zealand's Education System served Māori students and their *whānau*.

Over the next six months in 2016, I did some casual work with Jenny. Jenny was my good friend and mentor who I had met early in 2000 when I covered her teacher release at Te Mahoe. Jenny had left teaching and had started consultancy work in the field of supporting Neuro Diverse learners and professional development programmes for educators and schools. Jenny was someone I looked up to and admired and had successfully set up her consultancy business in Australia, working with several state schools. Jenny had always been a great motivator and encourager of me in pursuing the highest echelons of education. She also helped me navigate the space and mentored me while I was at Waiariki. With Jenny I felt free and in my element.

Daring to be brave to chase a PhD and home ownership

I loved going to her speaking presentations on teacher aide training around Northland and then I had to get a real job and taught for a term at Royal Oak Intermediate. It took a little adjusting for me to get used to not being the principal and I knew there was pressure from my former partner to get work to help cover expenses and add to the joint savings account. The holiday pay from Herekino was nearly finished, and I was basically at square one again. It was like being a first-year student at university. This external pressure could have deterred me, but it did not. I had to deal with it as best as I could. Being resourceful as I always am, I took out student loans and maxed out the visa to get my tuition fees paid. My former partner was very understanding during this time and helped with the visa card as later down the track he wanted us to get a mortgage.

In five years, I had been promoted from teacher to head of department and then to principal. We had only been married for five years and half of that time I lived up north. While I was away up north, there were flatmates at the apartment to supplement the rate of savings. I also had paid all my master's fees and again over four years that adds up to a lot of investment. I am the sort of person who loves learning and growing. I believed that within myself I owed it to fight for my dream of becoming the first in my family to embark on the PhD. A PhD is a huge milestone for a Māori. I was breaking glass ceilings and showing a way forward for the next generation that this Māori girl from Te Teko and Wairoa could do it. Money is an important aspect in any relationship and for my then former partner, it was always on the top of his agenda. In relationships, it's give and take. Sometimes I felt I lost my voice in conversation. That is never a good thing. A marriage is a commitment and very much like a PhD.

I had to negotiate and compromise with him about me doing my PhD. Although we were married, I needed to come to some sort of agreement that would keep him happy. I ended up applying for the Vice Chancellor's Scholarship that covered tuition and a tax-free stipend to the value of $100,000, and he had agreed that two days a week of teaching would be enough. We were renting a two-bedroom apartment which was reasonable at the time from an elderly couple in Freemans Bay. To supplement the difference, I also got a fixed term assistant teaching role at the University. I applied for Māori grants and scholarships to help pay for the other administrative tasks that come with studying a PhD.

Juggling a marriage, doing two part-time jobs, buying a home, and embarking on a full-time PhD programme was a mission. I got through it with a lot of long nights at the university. Yes, it meant sacrifice, but my new itch was to become a researcher and the latter homeowner. As you are doing a PhD, most people who surround you are unaware of the demands that come with doing one. I had left a decent principal's salary, and I would not be earning that sort of money again for another four years. I knew long-term that I needed to follow my passions and feel at peace with the direction I was taking in my career. Money does not make you happy. It provides an avenue for you to experience opportunities in life such as travelling, being able to go out to restaurants, and paying a mortgage.

In 2017 before I turned forty, we purchased our first home together in Papatoetoe. When hitting big milestones, I have often reflected on how far I'd come, parallel to my relationship. Buying a home is a major step and you should never feel compromised or be rushed into deciding. Talking through ideal locations, types of homes and the price of what you are willing to pay are important in joint decision making. I think you should never be pressured or give into demands to make the other person feel happy. Having respectful conversations means being able to listen to what the other person is saying and not taking it to heart just because other friends or colleagues have homes and rental properties and making comparisons to other people's lives. From my perspective, relationships are about making sure that both partners are all right with purchasing a home and taking the time and effort to collaborate with them, instead of isolating them into a corner.

When you are in a relationship, you do whatever it takes to get the deposit together to purchase a property. I used a substantial amount of my kiwisaver and my former partner used his savings and negotiated for a payout of his holiday pay from his employers alongside the joint savings we had accumulated. When I was at Te Kauwhata College in 2006, my colleague said to join two kiwisavers. A kiwisaver is a New Zealand saving scheme which had been operating around 2007 and was established to help with retirement and be used for first home deposit. So, since those years from Te Kauwhata I had been contributed to two schemes. At that stage of my life, I knew in the long-term it would be useful for my future financial security. While I was at Manurewa Intermediate School, a good friend introduced me to her husband, a Mortgage advisor at New Zealand Home Loans. Relationships matter. I need to be sure the people or groups I am working with can be trusted. As part of the administration work, we went together to the mortgage broker and after completing a series of questions we got a pre-approved mortgage based on our respective earnings as a couple. I had no permanent job and was feeling hesitant about how we would pay the mortgage as my relieving work was only casual and I had not been awarded my scholarship for the PhD. It took both the NZHL advisor and my former partner to convince me that my previous earnings as a principal would show the bank it would be possible for me to service with the scholarship and two days a week of casual relieving.

Once the pre-mortgage approval was affirmed, we started the house-hunting process. I think this is an area that should not be rushed, and the necessary time taken to both feel comfortable that it is the right home to purchase. We had been searching for a few months, and after some discussion, we settled on the property in Papatoetoe. I had not even considered or contemplated the thought of owning a home and having constant pressure placed on me. I caved into the demands. Auckland is a difficult market to get onto the property ladder if you do not have a 20% deposit and income and the servicing capability to take on the mortgage. However, it can be done and sometimes you must look outside the scope of where your desired location is. It is a bit of give and take and being realistic about what is affordable, and meeting compromises with the parties involved. It should not mean you are being pushed into decisions to purchase a home based on the fear of the other partner just wanting a home through emotional and mental turmoil.

We had been looking at homes in Ōtāhuhu and the real estate agent at the time suggested a place in Papatoetoe. I was not interested in it. Driving back to the city, we got into an argument and my former partner got out of the car and started walking away to the train station. I had to chase him to convince him to get into the car. Looking back, I should have put my foot down, but in a sense, I wanted to make him feel pleased and we ended up looking at the property. This is the home I did not fully like, but it took a lot of talking from my former partner and the NZHL advisor for me to get to a position and a mindset that it was a step onto the property ladder in Auckland. I had to allow control and trust in my former partner that it was his dream to have a property, and we jointly purchased it. After a few years in the home, I was further asked to think of taking out a mortgage to buy company shares in the business he was working for. I had completed three years of the PhD then and had agreed to consider this. I had an internal sense of feeling uneasy about the risk that would be involved in using the family home to support my former partner's dream of being a shareholder in a business he worked for. One week before a meeting was to take place, Covid hit the world. I was so glad that I held back on taking out the mortgage as COVID 19 disrupted the world we were living in for the next 18 months and would be a catalyst for the start of new beginnings.

6 KEY TIPS FROM CHAPTER 8:

1. In a relationship, talk through the process of buying a property.
2. Understand your partner and be open minded about having an in-depth conversation about future financial goals together. Do not push and rush a partner into big decisions.
3. At the onset of new stages of relationships, understand where each partner is coming from and get to know who they are, their dreams and values.
4. Work on the communication process with each other.
5. Tension is great in a relationship. It is how you work through communication together when it comes to addressing conflict and being willing to compromise as part of meeting halfway. If you have something to say, learn to collaborate with your partner and understand their perspective. Do not expect your partner to compromise their life values for your dreams!
6. Engage in *mahitahi* – collaborative practices. Work together as partners and be kind to your partner when moving through new challenges in life. Learn to listen to your partner and not force them into moves they are not ready for.

This chapter captures the journey of my life in growing from personal relationships and progressing in my career. Here is the breakdown of the key elements within the statement that revolves around the transformative nature of setbacks and triumphs. Let us break down the key elements:

I think the beginning statement shapes the essence of authentic leadership and the inner journey it entails. Let me break down what these key components are of authentic leadership:

1. ***Leading Authentically***:

    - The concept of authentic leadership implies a leadership style that is genuine, transparent, and true to oneself.
    - Authentic leaders prioritize sincerity in their actions and decisions.

2. ***Courage to Navigate Uncharted Territories***:

    - The use of 'uncharted territories within ourselves' suggests the exploration of aspects that may be unknown or less familiar.
    - Navigating these internal territories requires courage, indicating a willingness to confront and understand oneself deeply.

3. ***Using the Compass of Lived Experiences***:

    - The metaphor of a compass made up of lived experiences implies that the knowledge gained from past encounters serves as a guide.
    - Lived experiences become valuable tools for navigating challenges and making decisions.

4. ***Inner Journey of Self-Exploration***:

    - The notion of navigating uncharted territories within us implies a profound inner journey of self-exploration.
    - Authentic leaders actively engage in understanding their values, beliefs, and motivations.

5. *Application of Lived Wisdom:*

- The statement suggests that the wisdom gained from lived experiences is not just a passive collection of memories but an active compass.
- Leaders use this wisdom to make informed and authentic choices.

6. *Embracing Vulnerability and Self-Reflection:*

- The courage to navigate uncharted territories implies a willingness to embrace vulnerability.
- Authentic leaders engage in self-reflection and acknowledge their vulnerabilities as part of the leadership journey.

7. *Personal Growth and Development:*

- The use of 'uncharted territories' implies a continuous process of growth and development.
- Authentic leadership involves an ongoing commitment to learning and evolving based on internal exploration.

8. *Connecting Inner and Outer Worlds:*

- The compass of lived experiences serves as a bridge between the inner world of self-awareness and the outer world of leadership actions.
- Authentic leaders align their internal values with external leadership behaviours.

In summary, the dynamic and introspective nature of authentic leadership emphasises the courage to explore one's internal landscape, utilising the wisdom gained from lived experiences as a guiding compass. This approach fosters a leadership style that is grounded, sincere, and aligned with personal values.

> The most impactful leaders are those who draw from the well of their own challenges, turning adversity into empathy and compassion.

9

The Storm Before the Calm

Think before you act!

This is a common statement, but when actualised can become more than a handful of problems and serious earth-shaking. Problems are inevitable. It is a natural part of life. How you deal with problems can either bring out the best or worst in you. Problems go hand in hand with problem-solving and, as I have said earlier, the power of your decisions and behavioural actions can dismantle or enhance your life. We can all gain from being more self-aware of our emotions and learning strategies to control those emotions. Self-regulation of your emotions is important because it can help control your emotional state. Self-regulation involves understanding and controlling disruptive emotions and impulses, managing behaviour and reactions, and bouncing back from disappointment while staying true to your values. In this chapter, I take a deep dive into understanding how I learnt to navigate the storm of multiple challenges and come out the other side of the storm a better version of myself. But also, how you can develop your self-awareness and self-regulation skills as part of building emotional intelligence.

Sometimes, you can collapse under the pressure or tap into the source of *mauri* (life force) that lies within you. For Māori, *mauri* is the life force, that spark that lives inside of all living things and is passed down by your *tupuna* (ancestors) through *whakapapa*. The *mauri* contained within you can also be affected by *raruraru* (problem, dispute, conflict), if not addressed and resolved. It impacts one's *hauora* (wellbeing). Hence, it is never an easy task when dealing with people who bring *raruraru* into your life. Having the necessary faith, and *karakia* (prayer, Māori ritual), and being surrounded by *whānau* is a critical part of the healing process and falling forward rather than backward in turbulent times.

Getting married and buying a house together are powerful decisions that you make in life. Although there are circumstances that make it easier to decide for another, nothing has more power than the person pulling the trigger on the hardest decision that involves dismantling one's life and waiting for the tidal effect of pulling that trigger. Ignoring issues and not confronting matters with integrity is difficult, and living haphazardly is more than easy to do when procrastinating on one's indecisiveness. Speaking from experience, this indecisiveness means you are rather falling backward instead of falling forward.

Trials, unseen truths, tribulations, and celebrations

2022 was a big year for me. I got my secondment into an Early Career Academic (Māori) position at AUT and then I was helping my family in researching and preparing an application for enforcement of trustee obligations in the Māori Land Court. Māori Land Court allows registered landowners a place to be heard about the administration and management of Māori Land. Applications take time and often more than not are rarely heard unless there are serious issues at hand that can be addressed by the Judge of the court.

I had graduated as a Doctor in front of my family, and I did this with three other good friends, Māori nannies, Whaea Rose, Whaea Gloria and Whaea Jacqui who I got to know over my doctoral journey. This was an incredibly special time for me. The occasion humbled me as it was a lifetime dream of mine and what my *tipuna* would say, my destiny. Embarking on the PhD was realising a dream that I had set four years earlier after leaving my principal position. The PhD journey for me further strengthened my ties to *te ao Māori* and the role that I would play in my future. However, what I was to find out later in 2023 was to be the catalyst for further growth, change, and development in resetting and chasing my itch. But before I share that part of my story, I will take you back to the good memories I have of visiting Nanny Mei and being with our Waikato *whānau* at Te Teko Road.

When I was five, our parents would take us on our annual trip to Te Teko also known as Texas. We would stay at Nanny Mei's on Te Teko Road. Uncle George would be there and the *whānau* would all come over and we would have a great time together. The olds, that is our parent's generation, would be having a hearty garage party and if you have ever been to a party in Texas, you will understand what I am talking about. Lots of good times, singing, and plenty of glug, glug, glug. More often, that party would also head down to the local Te Teko Tavern. My dad would walk in first to the pub and then everyone was eyeing him up and wanting to fight this tall and skinny *Pākehā* (European). However, they did not realise who he was with and then the Waikato brothers, Uncle George and Uncle Boysie would follow in behind him and back him up. As kids while the olds were out at the pub or having a party in the garage, our older cousins would take care of us. That is Marina, Lorraine, Bubs, and Wharetini. Those would have to be some of the best times we spent together as cousins. See the Abraham kids we would come and hang out and often we would be mistaken for only being *Pākehā* until they realised who our mother was. Our Nanny Pie, Nanny Betty, and Nanny Mei always made us feel welcomed and loved. Nanny Mei would often spoil us with her pastries, mince pies, and sausage rolls she would bring home from work.

There is so much learning that can be gained from my dad's stories and my memories of times being in Te Teko. So let me break down some of the key elements of his stories and my memories:

1. ***Patron Interactions with Dad:*** The mention of Dad, a tall and skinny Pākehā, walking into the pub in the 1980s sets the scene. The anecdotes about patrons wanting to fight with him but not realizing who he was with, highlight a sense of surprise and the strength of unity within the family.

2. ***Support from the Waikato brothers:*** The support from Uncle George and Boysie, who would follow in behind my dad to back him up, highlights the importance of family solidarity and loyalty, especially in moments of potential conflict.

3. ***Older Cousins Taking Care of You:*** The memories of older cousins, Marina, Lorraine, Bubs, and Wharetini, taking care of you and the younger ones while the adults were out reflecting a sense of family responsibility and a bond between cousins.

4. ***Best Times Spent Together as Cousins:*** The acknowledgment that some of the best times were spent with cousins emphasises the joy and camaraderie within the extended family. Shared experiences during gatherings create lasting memories.

5. ***Identity and Recognition***: The mention of being mistaken for only being Pākehā until people realized who your mother was highlights the diversity within your family and the importance of recognizing cultural identity.

6. ***Welcoming and Loving Grandmothers:*** The presence of Nanny Pie, Nanny Betty, and Nanny Mei is portrayed as a source of warmth and love. The description of Nanny Mei spoiling you with pastries, mince pies, and sausage rolls adds a touch of familial care and affection.

7. ***Nurturing Atmosphere***: The narrative paints a picture of a nurturing atmosphere within the family, where care is extended not only by parents but also by older cousins and grandmothers. These moments contribute to a sense of belonging and security.

8. ***Culinary Memories***: The mention of Nanny Mei's pastries, mince pies, and sausage rolls creates a sensory element in the story, linking it to the shared experiences of enjoying homemade treats and the love embedded in them.

In summary, my interpretation of my dad's and my memories is a beautiful portrayal of family dynamics, support, and shared moments that create a tapestry of cherished memories. It reflects the importance of familial bonds, cultural identity, and the warmth of shared experiences.

Living with intent – Facing the pain and moving forward

A proportionate number of people take for granted how privileged we are in life. Sometimes, people will hide their true selves and only reveal their true intentions once the shit hits the fan. In 2023 there were big moments for me. It would have been easy to just give up and hide away in a corner to never be seen again or heard from. But something inside of me would not let me do that. My whole life, I had faced many challenges. I thought the Herekino story was the hardest, but the personal challenge of a failed marriage was to be one of the toughest periods in 2023. My connection to my people and the *whenua* (land) made a difference for me leading up to the events that were about to unfold before my eyes. But before that happened, I was commuting to Te Teko helping with getting the land case application to Māori Land Court and being there for my Uncle George.

Uncle George, one of my mother's brothers, was diagnosed with terminal cancer. Uncle George was a hearty man. He led his life authentically and did what he liked when he wanted. Everyone in Te Teko knew George and had respect for the man he was. Uncle had a PhD in life and had a love for his *Waikato whānau* and all his relations and friends. If you needed someone to cut down a tree, he was the man for the job. Uncle was always there, sitting on the doorstep with his girl, BumBum. Uncle George's whole world changed and being the man, it was only certain *whānau* were allowed to be close to him to support him on his final leg in this physical world we live in. I had the privilege to spend time with my uncle in doing his Māori land grants and supporting my sister, Caroline. What we do not realise is that life is short, and you must make the most of it. Sometimes, people cannot comprehend or consider other people's perspectives purely because of their narrow-mindedness and lack of integrity and character as human beings. Uncle George had the gift of bringing the community together, a natural charmer and shaker. He had the shopkeepers in Te Teko looking after him when he lived in Nanny Mei's homestead. Uncle George showed me so much in his last days of life here on earth and the importance of family and continuing to keep moving forward in difficult times. Although he was in pain, he showed strength and *mana* to others to live life to the fullest, no matter what is thrown at you. His *tangi* (funeral) exemplified to me how unity in families can be your greatest strength in facing collectively such painful times to help you move forward.

Navigating personal dilemmas in relationships

Before I get into the nitty-gritty of what I learnt from a failed relationship. It is worth taking the time to explain - What is a dilemma? A dilemma is a situation in which a person is faced with a difficult choice between two or more alternatives, where each option has both positive and negative aspects. The decision-maker may feel conflicted because choosing one option often means sacrificing something valuable associated with the other. Dilemmas can arise in various aspects of life, including moral, ethical, personal, or professional domains. Resolving a dilemma requires careful consideration of the consequences and values associated with each option, and it may involve making difficult trade-offs.

I believe I had been, like some people, living in a fog of mist, not oblivious to the state of reality that was happening around me. For the last year, I focused on triathlon training. I wanted to set my sights higher on something to aspire towards. This dedication and commitment to training meant I needed to do a lot of training with my tri buddies. Most of my time had been spent doing the things I enjoyed. I noticed a shift in the marriage, and we were struggling to communicate. I turned to my love for being active and spending time outdoors. I enjoyed being with my Iron Māori tri buddies. We all had a common vision to take care of our *hauora* (health and wellbeing) and collectively support each other as *whānau* while we were on the journey.

In March 2023, I travelled to Taupo for the weekend to compete in my first Taupo Half Ironman. I had committed to getting active, and in the process, I smashed another goal of mine which was finishing a half ironman. Ironman is important. It was always my dream to do one, so as part of building up to it, I did half the course. I swam 2 kilometres, cycled 90 kilometres, and then ran a 21 kilometre half marathon. I may have not been placed on the medal table, but I did not quit.

When I got home on Sunday, I had no idea what was going to unravel. The discerning look of my former partner showed something was seriously wrong and the tone of his voice when he came into the room while I was unpacking from the trip, he said to me, "We need to talk." From this point, I knew something was wrong and my worst fears had come true. Without getting ahead of myself, I sat still, like a stone, directly looking at him, whilst waiting to anticipate my line of inquiry and questioning of him.

As I came into the living room, my body knew that the situation was bad, and he had done something terrible. I sat down and asked him what the matter was and what he had done. His only words to me were "I fucked up." I was so angry with him for being dishonest, deceitful, and unkind to me, and in that moment, I accepted we were finished – *ka mutu*! From that point forward, I could never trust what would come out of his mouth and any explanation he gave me because of the litany of lies and entanglement that he got himself in and the impact this had on my *hauora* (wellbeing). The *patu ngākau* (trauma and wrongdoing) had a detrimental impact on my *hauora* and I was constantly questioning my worthiness as a human being and I realised I needed to change the version of myself that contributed to the destruction of the relationship. In hindsight, what had happened to me was a form of trauma which is an area that I had specialised in my PhD. I had a fair idea of the work that I now needed to do as part of healing from trauma. The first part of my healing process was acknowledging what had happened and the reality there was no going back but only forward. For me, it was about building a new future that my former partner would no longer be a part of.

There was no warmth from him towards me or care about how I was from my trip. It felt like all he wanted to do was to vomit out of his mouth the carnage he had created. He was looking at me with a sharp look of no feeling, and stone coldness. He had his usual glass of red wine in his hand sitting on the lazy boy. He had lied for so long and finally; I was going to get some part of the sordid truth for which

I was not prepared. I just lost it and came to a realisation, that all I wanted to do was to get the hell out of the room and get a divorce. I got in my car and drove off upset. I was extremely fortunate nothing happened to me. I was experiencing a rollercoaster of emotions. My head was all over the place, and I lost control of my emotions. I felt no semblance of order. I calmed myself down and made my way to my sister's and rang my dad along the way, who has always been my first point of call when I am in trouble.

When I look back over the last couple of years of the relationship, I had experienced so much stress from my former partner's drunken and disorderly behaviour. My head was at a standpoint and tired from the chronic worrying and the constant hurt I continuously was being bombarded with. I knew then that the relationship was finished and there was no comeback. I knew I deserved better. From about August 2022, my former partner would come home steaming and have his bag full of Hardy's One-litre red wine. I would watch him drink a litre of red wine in the evening, not knowing what was terribly wrong. I had asked if it were work, but to my unknown conscious it was more of the hidden pursuits, and the guilt I would say was eating him up. Patrick's drunken disorderly behaviour had always been there with my former partner, but I had accepted it as the norm. The late nights of coming home drunk and falling through the door's grill, his lack of knowing how he was getting bashed up or robbed on the streets and falling asleep on the Southern or Eastern Train in Auckland became more frequent.

It was the most soul-destroying moment of my life. I could never know what was to come. Sometimes in life, when you have no experience like what I was dealing with, you deal with matters differently. It is in the pain and loss that you learn for the next time how to better manage yourself. In challenging times, staying calm and keeping composure is not easy. It is important to acknowledge the feelings as part of the healing process. Drinking yourself merry helps in some respect, but it makes it harder to deal with the consequences. I owed it to myself to stay on the straight and narrow. Let me put it this way; you do what you need to do to deal with situations. Resetting also in these times requires the leader within you to step up to the plate. I know it is important not to hurt others and project onto them and to treat all people with respect, kindness, and care. However, in those moments of pain, you can also experience new ideas and learn from others how to find yourself again and deal with such damaging moments. I was so determined that I would not let this setback define me, but I was going to take the lead and do what I do best. Rise to the occasion and hold my head up. I needed to be reminded of who I was and where I come from. A leader with born traits to smash barriers, somehow, I had lost my footing, but I believe my spirit was being led by my *tupuna* to the place I was to be, which was strengthening my connections within *te ao Māori*.

Someone I had given 100% trust to, had not only betrayed me, deceived me, and disrespected me, made several decisions that undermined my sense of semblance and order in the world. The wisdom that comes from what I call a soul-destroying moment can either make or break you. It would have been easy to give up on me, but I have this fighter's attitude and I could not let such a soul-destroying moment define me. I could have easily fallen backwards but I did not. In the moment, I continued and kept fighting for a better future for myself.

Looking back over the last six months of 2023, I was so sequential in my manner of dealing with the breakup and the separation. I wasted no time and put my PhD skills and professional hat on. It only took a week to find legal advisors as I reached out to trusted associates about my situation. My trusted associates supported me to get my house in order. Of course, only you (the person impacted) can make decisions and the choice is in your hands with how your life would look like. Knowing the person I am, I was systematic in my approach to sorting the house we purchased together. I reached out to my family for help. As a family, we had been taught to be there for each other because once the elders are gone you must take the leadership role on and teach the next generation how to be family and to love each other without judgement.

In the second week, I found a financial advisor and a registered valuer. To get a pre-mortgage approval, I needed an actual valuation before the bank would give me an amount that I could borrow. The financial advisor showed me how I could get a better return on the income I had and looked at better ways of managing my investments and income. Sherlock (the family dog) and I had moved in with my other lifesaving sister and brother, who gave me a sense of order. Their unconditional support and their boys made an enormous difference in my healing. Sherlock Bones, my family dog, was so loyal. He was my *whangai* fur baby. Sherlock depended on me to take care of him, so every morning I would take him for a walk. This got me out of the house and took me back to the sea. I was extremely fortunate that my sister and her husband lived by the sea. So reconnecting back with nature also gave me much healing.

By the third week, I was setting a plan in motion to buy the family house. I had found a great mortgage broker who worked endlessly renewing my pre-mortgage approval three times over the six months. Sometimes things must happen the way they do. With set deadlines and targets to make, I knew time was not on my side. I was not going to let anyone get in my way. Ever so more determined, buying the house was not to be. What I have learned in my life is you can't control situations; you can only control your actions and you can't influence those who have caused the wrongdoing. I had to do what I needed to do and ended up interviewing real estate agents to sell the house and cleaning an entire house with the support of my sister.

When you set your mind to task especially me anything is possible. The *awhi* (support) that my sisters, Caroline, Julie and my brother Victor gave me made me further determined that I would not spend any more time wallowing in the gutter. Sometimes, the people you place your trust in can do the worst thing imaginable but not realise the devastation that they cause. It is during this painful time; that I chose to reflect and look at what I wanted from life.

I set a plan up with the support of my close family. I had mentally accepted life had to go on and falling forward was what I intended to do. I was firm in my direction, and I was not going to let anyone get in my way. If it meant sorting the house out by myself so, be it. In the entire process, of separation, you must put yourself first. My family was my lifeline, always there to support me when I needed help. When I needed a shoulder to cry on, I went to them. Being with my dad and connecting with nature at Mahia made me realise what was important to me and reminded me of who I was. The most invincible person who could do anything she wanted. The incident brought my family and me all closer together. I will be forever grateful to everyone who supported me on my journey to healing.

6 KEY TIPS FROM CHAPTER 9:

1. Push yourself harder than yesterday. Understand that reaching your potential does not happen overnight.
2. Be selective about relationships. Choose wisely.
3. Focus on endurance. It takes time to become successful.
4. Be generous to yourself, invest in learning and new experiences.
5. Aim to be your personal best every day. It takes time to heal from pain.
6. Be gentle with yourself.

This chapter captures the inner journey. Here is the breakdown of the key elements within the statement that revolves around the transformative nature of setbacks and triumphs. Let us break down the key elements:

1. Impactful Leaders: This phrase sets the stage by emphasizing the type of leaders being discussed—those who have a significant and positive effect on others and their environments.

2. Drawing from the Well of Challenges: This metaphor suggests that impactful leaders utilize their personal challenges as a source of insight and strength. Rather than being hindered by difficulties, they draw from these experiences as a valuable resource.

3. Turning Adversity into Empathy: The transformative aspect of leadership is highlighted here. Adversity becomes a catalyst for developing empathy, allowing leaders to better understand and connect with the struggles of others. This empathetic understanding is a powerful tool for effective leadership.

4. Turning Adversity into Compassion: In addition to empathy, impactful leaders also turn their challenges into compassion. Compassion involves not only understanding but also a desire to alleviate the suffering of others. It goes beyond empathy to active support and care.

5. Transformation of Challenges: The statement suggests that challenges are not viewed as roadblocks but as opportunities for growth and transformation. The adversity becomes a wellspring of qualities that enhance leadership effectiveness.

6. Personal Growth as a Leadership Tool: The idea presented implies that personal growth through overcoming challenges is not just for personal benefit but a tool for impactful leadership. Leaders who have faced and conquered challenges are often more resilient, adaptable, and understanding.

7. Connection with Others: The empathetic and compassionate leader connects more deeply with their team or followers. This connection fosters a positive and supportive environment, enhancing collaboration and productivity.

8. Resonance with Others' Struggles: Leaders who have navigated challenges are more likely to resonate with the struggles of those they lead. This shared understanding creates a sense of solidarity and trust within the team.

In summary, the most impactful leaders, according to the beginning statement, are those who have transformed personal challenges into empathy and compassion. By drawing from their well of adversity, these leaders not only grow personally but also become more effective in guiding and supporting others.

> Leadership is not about being immune to struggles; it's about using our lived experiences as a bridge to connect, empathize, and inspire positive change.

10
Getting back on track

Facing adversities in life

When you face adversity and challenges in your life, it takes time to work out what it is you are trying to achieve and, from my personal experience, you must confront those challenges head-on. So, a key point is whenever you are challenged or feeling down, you need to keep a positive mindset. Easy said than done, but it is possible to feel better by spending time rediscovering what your purpose is in life. Through deliberate intention, you must focus on yourself and keep the faith as part of reaffirming your purpose and direction in life. A side hustle to this is solving the biggest problem you may have.

So, work gave me something to look forward to and brought stability to my life. I refocused and started working towards my healing and redefining the pathway I would take for myself in my professional life. The encouragement of my two little sisters, Caroline, and Julie, kept me moving ahead. Both of my sisters work in remarkably high roles within corporate companies that advocate for diversity and inclusion for Māori. Their wise consul not only invigorated me but had me critically thinking about flying above the drama and not being dragged down into the gutters by ungrateful people like my former partner who was self-centred and determined to drag me through the mud.

I had decided that I needed to have my personal life in balance with my professional life. This involved setting some new dreams and goals and it involved working towards my promotion to become a senior academic. As part of realigning myself to my purpose, I looked at what was important to me, what did I enjoy doing and where did I want to head with my life. I set my mind firmly on becoming a professor and becoming the best researcher in my field related to my PhD. To become a better version of myself, I looked at how I could serve my community better in Te Teko and those communities that needed my help which was helping Māori students in accessing a university education pathway.

As a Māori academic I knew I could contribute positively to making a difference towards Māori students aspiring to go to university and be successful on their journey into university and at university. Everyone's journey is different. However, I will speak from my perspective as this is based on a true account of my lived experiences. We must remember that there are many ways to get into university, through the current schooling system or as an adult returning to studies. It had taken me at least a decade of hard work, sweat, and tears, and being in the right place at the right time to access and navigate the university system. A series of lifetime events and opportunities have allowed me the privilege to be where I am today.

Getting back on track and reaffirming your purpose and direction in life is a powerful and initiative-taking step toward personal growth and fulfilment. Here are some practical steps to help you in this process:

Reflection, Reset and Reenergise

1. ***Reflect on Your Values***: Consider the values that are most important to you. What principles guide your decisions and actions? Reflecting on your core values can help you align your life choices with what truly matters to you.

2. ***Revisit Your Goals***: Review your short-term and long-term goals. Are they still relevant to your aspirations and values? If necessary, adjust or set new goals that resonate with your current desires and ambitions.

3. ***Assess Your Passions***: Identify your passions and interests. What activities bring you joy and fulfilment? Reconnecting with your passions can reignite a sense of purpose and enthusiasm in your life.

4. ***Examine Your Current Path***: Evaluate your current trajectory. Are you satisfied with the direction you are heading? If not, consider what changes or adjustments might be necessary to align your path with your goals and values.

5. ***Learn from Setbacks***: if you have faced challenges or setbacks, view them as opportunities for growth and learning. Reflect on the lessons you have gained from these experiences and use them to inform your future decisions.

6. ***Seek Inspiration***: Look for inspiration in various forms, such as books, podcasts, mentors, or role models. Learning from others who have faced similar challenges and overcome them can provide valuable insights and motivation.

7. ***Create a Vision Board***: Visualize your goals and aspirations by creating a vision board. Include images, quotes, and symbols that represent the life you want to lead. Display it in a place where you can see it regularly.

8. ***Set Intentions***: Clarify your intentions for different aspects of your life, including relationships, career, health, and personal development. Setting intentions helps you stay focused on what matters most to you.

9. ***Develop a Plan:*** Break down your larger goals into actionable steps. Create a realistic and achievable plan to work toward your objectives. This can help you regain a sense of control and progress.

10. ***Practice Mindfulness:*** Incorporate mindfulness practices into your routine. Mindfulness can help you stay present, reduce stress, and gain clarity on your thoughts and emotions.

11. **Connect with Supportive People:** Surround yourself with positive and supportive individuals who understand your journey and encourage your growth. Share your aspirations with them and seek their guidance.

12. **Celebrate Small Wins:** Acknowledge and celebrate your achievements, no matter how small. Recognizing your progress can boost your confidence and motivation to continue moving forward.

Remember, reaffirming your purpose and direction is ongoing. Life is dynamic, and your goals and values may evolve. Regular self-reflection and adjustments to your path are key to staying aligned with your true self and finding lasting fulfilment.

Education for Māori in Aotearoa New Zealand

For many Māori students, staying in the main flow of the *awa* (river) is not easy in New Zealand's mainstream education system. But with the right support mechanisms and structures in the Western Academy, alongside *whānau, hapū* (sub-tribe), Māori organisations and tribal support, Māori can achieve educational success as Māori. So, understanding success is built upon a solid platform of many steps in an individual's journey through schooling and in life.

The early years of schooling and education in the home are vital to one's success. A family that encourages and promotes education is already ahead of the game. Children grow up observing and learning from their parents within the home. Exposure to authentic learning can shape a child's outlook on life. I have categorized the learning stages into year groups for ease of explanation of what parents and families can consider helping children grow into lifelong learners.

Engaging in lifelong learning is a process that allows a child to grow and be nurtured into the education space that begins with the family. What is important for a Māori student's success is having constant and committed support from family. That is having love and attention poured into *rangatahi* (young children/teens) and making them feel validated and worthy of greater success. The warmth and positivity of family can leave the biggest imprint on a student's self-belief and confidence to do well at school and later as they choose to enter university.

Here are some steps below that make a difference in supporting Māori to be successful in attaining educational success at different stages of their life. Now it must be noted that you can start anywhere on the spectrum after 20 years of age to study at university and for myself, I started studying a PhD at the age of thirty-six. Some points that I have noted during my time navigating mainstream education and completing a doctoral programme about the different learning stages for a Māori student:

Conception to 4 years old

- Reading daily to children from a range of literacy sources.
- Singing *waiata* (songs) to children and playing music.
- Walking and playing in nature and the environment.
- Taking children on holiday to learn about their *marae* and spending time with *whānau*.
- Attending preschool, kindergarten or *kohanga* (Māori early childhood centre).

5-10 years old

- Reading daily.
- Having family conversations at the dinner table.

- Practising times tables and additions.
- Learning sight words.
- Teaching children about their *whakapapa* and meeting their grandparents and important cultural landmarks.
- Speaking *Te reo Māori* (Māori language) to children and incorporating language into conversation.
- Attending primary school and joining in-class activities and team sports for social development.

11-17 years old

- Scheduling time aside to study.
- Complete homework set aside from class.
- Learn how to revise and make notes for study.
- Attending intermediate school.
- Attending college or secondary school.
- A pre-requisite is for students to pass NCEA Level 1-3.

18 – 21 years (Undergraduate – Bachelor degrees, Diploma and Certificate programmes)

- Complete an undergraduate degree.
- Join a sports team.
- Attend additional learning classes for student support – APA referencing, writing support.
- Find part-time work as an undergraduate to supplement living and learning costs for studying.

22-24 years (Postgraduate – Bachelors with Honours/Masters)

- Select an area to study in that is specialized.
- Apply for student scholarships from both Pākehā and Māori organisations.

- Think of an idea that you wish to study for your thesis.
- Choose a research paper as part of your masters programme as this sets you up for completing a PhD later on if you decide to pursue it.
- A+ average to attain a doctoral scholarship to help fund your university studies.

25 – 29 years (Doctoral studies) – but it can be done at a later stage of life too!

- Each university has their requirements and criteria for completing a PhD.
- Locate the university you want to attend and the possible list of supervisors.
- Undertake a research proposal, a candidature proposal, and ethics application to be granted access into the doctoral programme.
- Secure two/three supervisors to take care of you over the 3–4-year period.
- Embark on a training programme to help you balance your life.
- Get involved in the university life and make lots of new friends.

30 – 35 years Early career academic (ECA)

- Life after graduating starts with looking for work or further opportunity to advance in the university.
- Align yourself with a group who value you and it may mean taking a job to get a foot in the door.
- Balance your portfolio of teaching, research, and community service in the first years and have a go at applying for research grants.

- Develop publications and speak about your research as part of building your portfolio for assessment.

To succeed as Māori at University

Understanding the historical framing of education for Māori in Aotearoa New Zealand is needed to acknowledge the trauma that has been intergenerationally been passed down through generations of *whānau*. From my personal experience, the journey to graduating as a 'first in family' with a doctoral degree known as a PhD, is a rare event. It is a celebration of change and empowerment! It means I have broken the intergenerational cycle for my family, my *hapū* and my *iwi* (tribe). I have proven with the support of both the metaphysical and physical worlds that we live in is that if I can do it, other *whānau* can do it! My mother and father are proof that hard knocks can only make you stronger. My dual worldview as being both *tangata tiriti* (people who came after the Treaty of Waitangi) and *tangata whenua* (the people of the land) informs my thinking and perspectives of life.

Over the four years I was studying my PhD, I rarely saw or had Māori friends doing a PhD except for the three *kuia* (nannies) I came across in my second year of the four-year journey. I had to grow a thick skin and be accustomed to organisational dilemmas and the demands of a Eurocentric system that showed a lack of empathy for Māori educational success. But as time went by over the four years, I was a Māori doctoral candidate I saw shifts in the university. These shifts saw a change in the organizational culture, that is the landscape of how education is supposed to empower and transform communities that I as 'the individual' came from, Māori.

To progress at university, you must be dedicated, disciplined, and consistent with your daily habits. By building on your habits, it is possible to progress from your undergraduate degree to masters and eventually to your doctoral degree known as a PhD. Doing a PhD means being disciplined and committed to your studies. It is vital to stay on track and when things happen access the necessary support. It may even mean taking a break from studies and coming back to the PhD later. However, life happens, and you just must make sure that your supervisors are aware of the things that are happening in your life.

I have progressed through every stage of New Zealand's education system, jumping hoops and sky-passing teachers who had little belief in my abilities to succeed. Being Māori and having the financial capability to stay at university is incredibly challenging. I owe a lot of my success to my dad. My dad was selfless. He worked double jobs to help me with university. My dad helped me in my first three years at university. Not only was he an inspiration, but our dad also raised four children to become great human beings, responsible members of society who care for and serve people, our communities. Dad gave us the tools to survive on our own and stand on our own two feet.

Through mentoring and a supportive and nurturing environment in my faculty and within my team I was always encouraged and supported to apply for DCT contestable funding. Through people believing in me and helping me to take the next step into the unknown opportunity I was successful in securing two funding grants totalling $100k. This extra push has allowed me to work with amazing people across two faculties at AUT who are passionate and really care about transforming STEAM education that better supports Māori and Pacific learners into postgraduate studies within the fields of Science, Technology, Engineering, Arts, and Mathematics (STEAM). The second project also has allowed me to really delve deeper into how Artificial Intelligence (AI) can be responsibly used to respect a Māori worldview, and transform the educational landscape in Aotearoa New Zealand.

I have developed a wheel that highlights key stages and skills that an individual develops while learning to be successful at university. It is a cyclical formula that can be applied to your pathway at university. University is so much different from secondary schooling. The transition from schooling is another leap up. Time management, goal setting, and reflection are key skills to master if you want to be successful at university.

Preparing for success to engage in university education

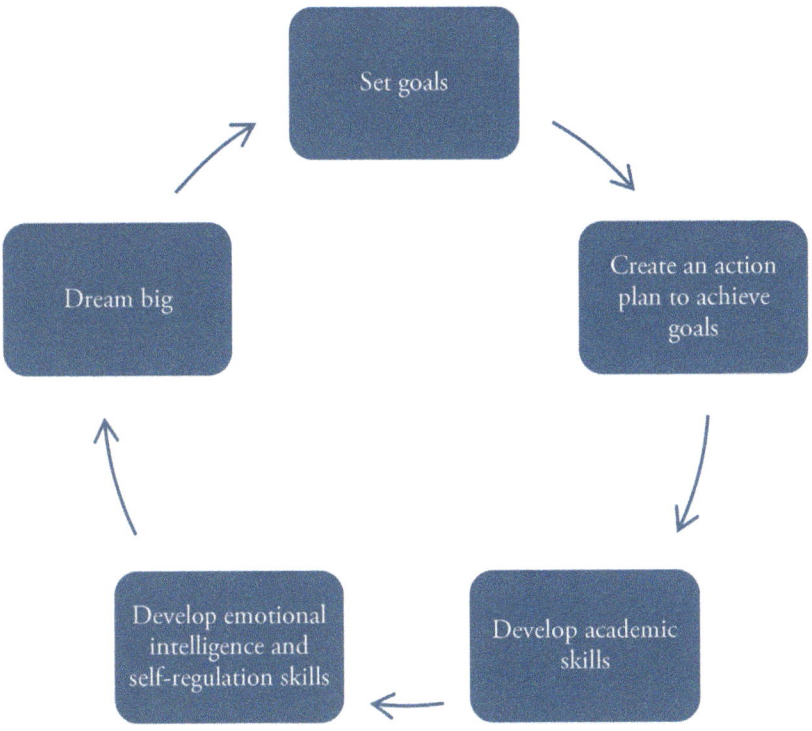

Dream big!

Develop a vision board of all the things you want to achieve. This will help you to visualise what it is that you want to do with your life. In this phase, you think about what you want to achieve, and who will benefit from your success. Dreaming about how successful you will be is about uplifting yourself. It means developing a strong growth mindset that will raise your beliefs internally within, that you can achieve something great, and you are worthy of success.

Set goals

Here you write what goal(s) will help you achieve your dream and give you direction in life. I have often found the use of the Specific, Measurable, Achievable, Relevant, and Time-Bound (SMART) goal method useful as I navigated both the schooling system and university. SMART goals give a criteria to guide in the setting of goals and tasks that are aimed at helping you to become successful. Writing your goals down helps you to become accountable and helps you to set in motion the direction you want to go in life and what you want to accomplish.

Create an action plan to achieve your goals

A goal is a signpost like a milestone that you can use to check one's progress. A part of setting your goals includes activating prior knowledge about the difficulty of the task and one's ability in an area. An action plan lists the goals and the set tasks that will help you to achieve the goal. The first part is being specific about what you want to achieve. From here, you then list the tasks and activities you must complete to achieve the goal. The next step is to identify the critical tasks and assign each task with a date that it will be completed. If you need support, then assign tasks to individuals where necessary.

Develop your academic skills

As part of your journey, it is important to do the workshops that are offered by the university, such as developing your American Psychological Association (APA) referencing skills and learning to paraphrase and write academically. When you emphasize the practical skills that will assist you in your studies, such as academic writing, learning to paraphrase, and critically examine reading materials it will grow your belief in yourself.

Develop your emotional intelligence and self-regulation skills!

As an individual, you need to learn how to keep your emotions, and your feelings, in check. Often referred to as emotional intelligence and includes self-regulation. Self-regulation development involves understanding one's beliefs and ability to be successful. As an educator, we need to support students to learn to focus one's energy and attention on the task at hand. Examples of attention-focus strategies involve being in stillness, removing distractions from your study space, maybe visiting the library or study rooms, and postponing enjoyable activities to make progress towards one's goals.

From my perspective, emotional intelligence is the ability to perceive, interpret, evaluate, and control your feelings when you communicate and interrelate with others. Sometimes, depending on the situation or event that has caused you stress, the stress of a situation can rock your world. It is important to recognise your triggers, particularly when you are feeling under duress and in stressful situations. What you can think about here is observing and discerning how individuals treat you, communicate with you, and relate to you. When under stress, the mind can often wander if you allow it to. So, recognise the different types of feelings you have and learn some strategies to maintain balance in your life when you are under stress from life. Emotional intelligence also involves how you respond to the emotions of others. From my experiences and opportunities in life, I have learned to become more adept at developing my emotional intelligence. Here are some examples:

- Having a sixth sense of being able to identify and describe what people are feeling.
- Being aware of your strengths and weaknesses, often knowing what your limitations are.
- Look inward at yourself and build your self-confidence and self-acceptance. Self-acceptance for me is about loving yourself and accepting yourself. Through self-compassion, you can learn to let go of mistakes and take responsibility for your mistakes.
- Thinking before you act. Take the time to listen and be patient. Assessing the situation before responding. You must learn to let matters go and keep moving ahead.

6 KEY TIPS FROM CHAPTER 10:

1. To be a good student takes time, commitment, and a supportive environment.
2. Learning to not stop and aim high at university; never settle for anything less than what you deserve.
3. A supportive family and finances are needed to help Māori participate in higher education.
4. Sacrifice is a necessary component of being successful at university.
5. Helping others once you have completed a PhD is part of the process of building sustainability and capabilities for Māori to reach the highest levels - Professor.
6. Your *whānau* are the best supporters of your success; build others up as you progress through the education system in Aotearoa New Zealand.

This chapter captures the journey of prioritising yourself, developing your authenticity, connection and positive impact on people and the environment. Here is the breakdown of the key elements within the beginning statement at the start of the chapter that revolves around the transformative nature of setbacks and triumphs. Let's delve into the key elements:

1. *Leadership and Struggles*:

- The acknowledgment that leadership is not about being immune to struggles challenges the idea of leadership as a position of invulnerability.
- It recognizes that leaders, like everyone else, face challenges and difficulties.

2. ***Lived Experiences as a Bridge***:

    - The metaphor of lived experiences as a bridge implies a connection between the leader and those they lead.
    - It suggests that personal experiences become a pathway for understanding, relating, and building connections.

3. ***Connecting Through Empathy***:

    - The use of the term 'bridge to connect' emphasizes the role of empathy in leadership.
    - Leaders who draw on their lived experiences can empathize with the experiences of others, fostering a deeper understanding.

4. ***Inspiring Positive Change***:

    - The statement underscores that leadership is not just about understanding but about inspiring positive change.
    - By leveraging their own experiences, leaders can motivate and guide others toward positive transformations.

5. ***Authenticity in Leadership***:

    - The idea that leaders use their lived experiences as a bridge highlights the importance of authenticity.
    - Authentic leaders are open about their own journeys, creating a transparent and genuine leadership style.

6. *Humanizing Leadership*:

- The concept challenges the perception of leaders as detached figures by emphasizing their shared human experiences.
- It humanizes leadership, making it more relatable and accessible to those being led.

7. *Building Trust and Connection*:

- Sharing lived experiences builds trust and connection within a team or organization.
- It establishes a foundation of trust, as team members see their leader as someone who understands and empathizes with their challenges.

8. *Catalyzing Positive Change*:

- The emphasis on inspiring positive change suggests that leadership is a catalyst for improvement and growth.
- Leaders become agents of positive transformation, motivating others to strive for better outcomes.

In summary, being empathetic is a key aspect of authentic leadership. By using lived experiences as a bridge, leaders can connect on a deeper level with their teams, foster empathy, and inspire positive change, creating a leadership style that is impactful and transformative.

> Toitu te whānau hitori.
>
> (Honour family histories)

11

Strengthening connections to *te ao Māori* (Māori world)

Know your whakapapa

Understanding the *whakapapa* of my ancestors was an important step in being able to access land grants and scholarships that are connected to one's *whakapapa* for the sole use of supporting educational advancement. Starting with identifying your parents and grandparents' lines will help with accessing grants for higher education and secondary education that may include stationary and uniform costs for schooling and sometimes accommodation costs for boarding school.

To identify land blocks begins with doing a rigorous search through Māori land courts online data base. At every major centre there is a regional office where Māori can go and search for *whakapapa* related to the minute book records of how Māori achieved succession from genealogy links or through gifted donees. Knowing who you are can help with strengthening your connection to the *whenua* and to the ancient knowledge of our ancestors.

Another area to access funding is registering on major tribal areas that you are connected to through *whakapapa* and as *whangai* (Māori adoption into the family). As I was doing my PhD I was completing further successions to my ancestors on behalf of my mother's generation. For many years I looked and reviewed the documentation at Māori Land Court and tracked that many of our *tupuna* had not been succeeded to since the Māori Land Court came into conception in 1865.

More recently I gained three important *tamoko* (Māori tattoo) that acknowledged the ancestors and my family. A *tamoko* is further alignment to my purpose and strengthening my connections within *te ao Māori*. The importance of my *whakapapa* reminds me of who I am and where I have come from as part of my journey to reach further success and become the best version of myself. Taratoa the

Strengthening connections to *te ao Māori* (Māori world)

tamoko artist I chose was from Ruatoki and came from a line of *tohunga* (proficient expert) *tamoko* artists. I had been wanting to start my new life and pathway with realigning with the things that matter the most to me. *Whānau* and *whakapapa* go hand in hand, and it is with much honour I share the final artefacts that were designed on a shared understanding of *wānanga* (discussion, talk and deliberating) between myself and Taratoa. At each of the sittings, we did *karakia* and these sessions were staggered over the last three months of 2023. My new *taonga* (treasures) further validify my rightful space to wear *tamoko* as a *wahine* (women) but it was also a healing process for me with my ancestors.

6 KEY TIPS FROM CHAPTER 11:

1. Honour *whakapapa* and *whānau*.
2. Be true to yourself and your journey.
3. Be prepared for your *tamoko*, get the *whakapapa* together and share this with the *tamoko* artist.
4. Always return to your *turangawaewae* as many times as you can.
5. Stay true to your journey; sometimes you have to leave others behind as they no longer align with your values and way of being.
6. Never let anyone diminish your *mana*. Own your *mana* and remember who you are and where you come from.

I have used various sources to regain unknown *whakapapa* as part of my journey to strengthen my connections within *te ao Māori*. *Whakapapa* connects us to the environment and to the metaphysical world, our *tupuna*. For Māori, going back to your elders to learn about your *whakapapa* is a rite of passage, but as I learnt, it was a necessary part of understanding what my true purpose was in life. My doctoral studies lead me to learning more of the *whakapapa* and the rich narratives of where my people, my place of belonging centres in Te Teko as part of strengthening my connections to *te ao Māori*.

The final stage that made a difference for me when I started my doctoral journey was learning about who I was as Māori. It began with going back to my *turangawaewae* (my place or roots of belonging) and meeting with *kaumātua* to learn about my *Whakapapa*. Learning about *whakapapa* grows you as a person and it is a journey that continues to further take place within the space of *mātauranga Māori*.

Strengthening connections to *te ao Māori* (Māori world)

The connections of my ancestors to the *whenua* are rooted in the rich histories of my Waikato *whānau*, who are descendants of a *rangatira* line that is central to the little rural town of Te Teko. Here I take you on a journey of learning about an important Māori community that is taken for granted by western society who often frown upon my people. The context and background will help you understand the significance of knowing who you are as Māori and as part of forming your cultural identity (See Appendix 1). I acknowledge that this chapter comes from my doctoral thesis – Iti noa ana, he pito mata: A critical analysis of educational success through a Māori lens and two case studies of whānau from Ngāti Awa and Ngāti Tūwharetoa.

> Learn to prioritise yourself, your own happiness, because if you do not, no one else will.

12
The power of new adventures

Learning to accept and love yourself unconditionally entails discovering who you are and reviewing and resetting your boundaries. I have found that being gentle with myself includes reframing my self-talk and honouring my alone time as part of healing from the soul wounds caused by traumatic experiences. Healing from your soul wounds includes letting go of resentment, that built-up anger that comes from people hurting you. I have found that it is essential to protect your peace from those people who want to pull you down instead of elevating you to become a better person. As part of the healing journey, work with your community to work out a plan for healing and begin to be strategic with the people you spend time with. Spend time with people who love you and genuinely care about you.

Getting closure from a relationship is never easy. Acknowledging and accepting that the relationship is over is your first step to recovery. It is human nature to get upset after a breakup. The dreams you once had, and the potential of that relationship are gone. It does not matter what's happened; it's how you allow yourself to react and to be influenced by it all. You can only control your emotions and influence others by your choice of words and actions. You have no control over how people react and how they respond to your influence. A breakup teaches you more about yourself and how you can take the opportunity to rewrite your canvas from white to the most colourful palette for your future.

So here are some little steps to success to get you moving along from a breakup. Hopefully, you can take some lessons about taking care of yourself or others who may be in a similar situation.

Step 1: Make yourself a priority!

Prioritizing yourself is difficult if you have neglected this over time or while being in a long-term relationship. Putting yourself first is not selfish. It is real; and organic. It involves focusing on developing new habits of nurturing oneself in developing into one's true self. When you are beginning the healing process this includes acknowledging and accepting the raw deal that the relationship is over. It is an opportunity to bring a bit more colour and peace to your life. The healing process can only start with you! When the timing is right, acknowledgement and acceptance go hand in hand. I entered a stage of discovery and rediscovering the things, the new habits that nourish my soul, my world. I believe that investing in myself, being selfish with me, was the best action that I had done in 2023. Prioritizing myself, putting me first before others' needs has allowed me to flourish into a better version of myself and identify what I genuinely wanted in life. I have taken the time to care about my mind, my soul, and my spirit; by working on me!

Step 2: Define your needs

What is essential to survive and work through resetting new goals. Remember, keep everything simple. K.I.S.S (Keep It Simple Stupid). Get into your physical fitness and start training for some big event that you have never done. Even better reset with a personal trainer (PT). PT trainers are fantastic people who believe in helping people to reach their own health goals. I had the opportunity to train for ALTA, a mixed martial arts training programme where you are with the top coaches at City Kickboxing. I needed to smash a few pads and get into my fitness, and I saw training for a fight was the best way forward. Training with the boys helped me to push myself outside my comfort zone to become fitter and mentally stronger. Being in an environment that was so supportive and where people shared the same values of doing better and helping others had made a difference to my *hauora* (health and well-being). I felt like I was getting back to myself and feeling better inside of me.

The ethos around working hard, challenging yourself, and growing was evident while training at City Kickboxing. My ritual for about 13 weeks of the 20-week programme was to get up at 5:30 am and be at training at 6:45am. I never wanted to turn up late as the Coach would call you out and dish out a penalty. The people who were training for ALTA were very encouraging and helpful to newbies like me. The sparring sessions became my favourite part of training as we could put our new skills to the test. I was matched up with the boys who were within the same weight range as myself. I had some good one-on-one sparring hits and was not scared to take a knock from the boys and give them a few punches and kicks back. However, during a sparring session heading into the final run-up to the ALTA event, I got taken down by one of the boys, which meant my time was cut short. After a couple of days and getting medical attention, I had torn my meniscus ligament and the patella ligament. When these get injured, you miss having the ability to stretch and bend your knee. Injuries teach you to be very patient. Something that has grown on me over the years.

Step 3: Set boundaries around time and who has access to you!

When I prioritised what is of value, and who I enjoy being around, that is where I saw the greatest shift in me. In nine months, I had focused on setting boundaries around my time and space. Training was a high priority for me. I was training 2-3 times a day for 5-6 days of the week as part of the ALTA programme being run at City Kickboxing, attending regular personal training sessions with Mia, and going to Hybrid training at Fort Knox 4-6 times of the week. I enjoyed Hybrid training in the evenings as I was becoming conditioned as a fighter. The same culture that existed at City Kickboxing was also embedded with the Hybrid crew.

After the initial consultation with the specialist orthopaedic doctor, I struggled with my injury and was forced to completely stop all forms of training for eight weeks. Doing no training made me frustrated, but I had to listen to the specialist if I wanted my ligament to heal. My body needed to rest and effectively I needed to slow down and learn to be ok by myself. In the eight weeks I walked around with a huge brace that just had my right leg locked. So, I made the most of the time and learned to have a little bit of downtime, going out and catching up with friends, enjoying the occasional drink, and trying out new restaurants in Auckland. Setting time aside to visit my brother in Brisbane was one of my highlights of 2023. I loved South Bank and at the time was very tempted to stay and not return. Brisbane is a great city and has a good vibe for going out drinking, shopping, and dining. However, I had to come back to Auckland and begin sorting the sale of the house and finalise the separation.

Step 4: Stop beating yourself up – learn to be kind to yourself!

The reason we can be so hard on ourselves is that the person who has done the wrongdoing towards you has shown that you have compromised your values. So, for me, it was important to show self-compassion and self-forgiveness as part of healing from the shame and guilt that comes from being betrayed by a partner. The same kindness I showed to my friends was what I needed to do for myself. Self-forgiveness is the action I took to release the pain of an embarrassing action and the distressing situation in which my former partner had created chaos for me and the biggest problem I needed to resolve immediately.

Learning to forgive is about letting go of the guilt and shame associated with the situation that is causing pain for you. Learning to forgive myself has been part of re-discovering who I am. I had to learn to not be so hard on myself and not take on my shoulders the chaos created by my former partner. I had to reset myself and start rebuilding myself into a happier person. My former partner's actions and treatment towards me made me feel the lowest I ever had in my life. It hit me hard when he went awol, missing for two weeks. I had no closure to resolving the issue like adults. Be aware of destructive habits that you may use to deal with situations such as the use of alcohol to numb your pain. Just be sure that you do not become entangled in using alcohol to compensate for your grief. The steps I had to take over the last nine months of 2023 included working on my self-talk and rejigging my mindset, which included acknowledging it is all right to make mistakes and learn from these. Another habit involved getting real with myself and honestly looking at myself and understanding what I was upset about. Taking corrective action and repairing the damage I may have caused to others as part of closing a door on a stage of my life and regaining perspective.

What I can say from the breakdown of my marriage was a blessing. I have become stronger, and more aware of what I wanted for my life. I may not have seen it nine months ago, but the separation had provided me with the most personal transformation ever. I had experienced something so horrible, but beautiful. I owed a lot to my family, my little sisters, my big brother, my dad, and my mum for being on call 24/7 and my beautiful nephews for bringing life back to me and helping me to get back on my feet. There were also my beautiful friends, both near and far from New Zealand, who were there for me. My remarkably close friends came to my aid at the drop of a pin. These friends epitomise the values I stand for integrity, honour, and *whakamana* (being uplifting) people. We all share the values of *tika* (doing the right thing and being genuine), *pono* (being honest), and *aroha* (having empathy and showing kindness). If ever I needed something, they were there. We laughed, we drank, and better - they carried me when my wings were broken.

After the first day of breaking up, my sister would not allow me to stay at our home in Papatoetoe. She told me to get in the car and pack my bags and I was coming to live with her husband and family. I was so lost in transition, not knowing what I was going to do. My mental health was off the Richter scale. I was incredibly angry and disorientated. I was questioning my sanity as to how I could have contributed to the situation. I was so mad that I had placed all his belongings in rubbish bags and left them outside the house. I can now laugh at this, but at the time, it felt like madness. Sometimes external support is needed to get things moving along. All communication lines had been severed between both of us. Sometimes, having no contact is needed as part of the healing process.

Another avenue that helps with walking through a breakup is going to counselling. Everyone is different and counselling may not be for everyone. For me, counselling allowed me the space to talk about my feelings and speak to someone without judgment. You are talking to someone about your problems, trying to find some sense of semblance of order.

Your family, are also there to listen to you. *Whānau rongoa* (family as healing) can be your greatest strength in helping you move forward. Going back to Te Teko and Wairoa and connecting with *whānau* gave me something to look forward to and appreciate all the positive things that I had in life and reminded me I am loved unconditionally.

What I can say is having my other good friends who knew me before being married made a huge difference and they know who they are. Friends I had not seen for decades offered me a place to live and resettle to take a break.

So, the moral of the story is to reach out and do not be alone in these difficult times. Feeling guilty is ok but do not hang onto this feeling. Acknowledging aloud it is alright to make mistakes is a part of learning and growing into a better version of yourself. Recognising that learning to move on takes time and having patience with oneself is essential to developing a positive outlook on life. This difficult spot you are in from separation and betrayal is not permanent, but sometimes we can get wrapped up in the emotions that we need to learn how to keep calm under pressure. Something that I learned when I did Dave's workshop at Piha was taking control of your breathing and thoughts to manage your emotions. Breathing in and exhaling out can make a huge difference in settling the mind, bringing you back down to earth, and finding your rhythm again.

Step 5 – Learning to live by your values and set boundaries in relationships.

It is important to say no to people and live more by your values. I am louder than ever at being forefront of my beliefs. I will not compromise my values and what I stand for. The bullocks you may have experienced from negative people has no place in your life. Articulating out aloud is easier than we think. I had enough of the separation back and forth that I had to put my foot down with lawyers, the real estate agent, and the former partner. Nobody speaks for me and can take away my voice. Standing my ground and being firm is something of which I am immensely proud. If you have something to say, then say it. I have never been louder than I had in the last few months in 2023, dealing with real estate companies and agents that do not align with your values of *tika* (doing right), *pono* (being genuine and honest), and *aroha* (showing empathy). It is easy for people to say something but actions speak louder than words. I'm stepping up more and calling out wrongdoing because our world and society need more caring and empathy from each other.

Step 6 – Try new things

I attended a range of Yoga relaxation calming classes, going tramping in the bush at Waipu and dying my hair in many different colours. Going waka pink was a bit drastic, but it was fun walking into the hairdressers in Wellington and letting her do such a wild colour I had never done. I think training and sparring in mixed martial arts (MMA) was one of my favourite things to try. I enjoyed the mass training together and getting up early in the morning. It gave my mind something else to think about than dealing with the separation and clearing out a house by myself. While I am sitting here writing away, compiling my first-ever book is another new thing that I have done that brings joy to my life. I love to talk, and writing is now becoming a full-on passion. I believe that writing has allowed me to share my voice and, in turn that voice may lift someone out of despair. Having fun has also meant building new connections and meeting amazing people at work and through my research connections. Spending more time on my passions, such as attending drama performances, fashion and beauty, and getting into scuba diving has empowered me to *(re)focus*, *(re)set*, and *(re)energize* myself thus overfilling my cup of happiness. I have found another new world to thrive in with scuba and experience calmness from swimming underneath the ocean and water life. The Poor Knights and Cathedral Cove have been eye opening experiences and amazing places to visit in New Zealand. Once, you visit you will realise why it is necessary to do on anyone's wish list.

Step 7 – Indulge yourself and be with others

I have set time aside to appreciate myself better. I have redefined my vision and pathway in life by collaborating with new advisors and mentors to establish my business, Auahatia – Innovate with Hazel, alongside developing my research career. Juggling a business and a career is huge on its own. But I have learned that getting others in to help with the balance has been an awakening. I am excited that within six months, I have set up a platform by authoring my first book to share my experiences with other women and professionals who are aspiring to attain leadership roles and chase their dreams. On the other side to this indulging is spending more time to take care of myself such as regular hair and nail spa days every 6 weeks, foot pedicures, and doing personal training sessions with Mia. What I have learned is you must spend more time with yourself to understand what you want in life and what you are not willing to compromise or bend over for somebody.

6 KEY TIPS FROM CHAPTER 12:

1. Practise self-care and self-love.
2. Remember not to compromise your values.
3. Practise self-compassion like you would do with friends.
4. Prioritise your time and the space you are in.
5. Live life and go out with friends to new events.
6. Feel pain and learn to let go of it.

In this chapter, I share my insights into key steps for making myself a priority and setting out on new adventures. I share three life stories of the different activities that I have done to challenge myself to become a better person. This is training for my first fight night, training for a half ironman and training for Alta, a mixed martial art fight like the UFC. Of course, it is never easy to train for any of these physical events, but it is daring to grow as a person. I have a love for learning and during my years I have come to love spending time with likeminded people who have a passion for wellbeing and life.

13
Guide points for life

There is no right way to live your life. Learn to embrace yourself and write/rewrite your histories from experiences. Through the positive and negative experiences of life, we can grow; however, if you do not learn from your mistakes, the universe will keep challenging you until you realise that your habits and patterns must change to reach the best version of yourself. Know your fears, address these self-doubts of unworthiness, and accept that you are worthy. Not everyone is meant to stay in your life; sometimes they are there for you to learn a little bit more about yourself.

How we live our lives is down to ourselves. We imitate what we see and learn as children from our parents. Our first teachers in life. Over time, we grow up, go to school, do our primary and secondary education, and maybe enter university or start our adult life off with getting a job or an occupation, or even take a risk and set up a business. The work friends and people you met along the way are going to take from you or lift you. So, it is important to understand finding the right mob for you. A mob is your people, and they are truly the people who care, love you, and bring peace to your world, not take from your world. But what I will say is you need those people who pretend to be your mob to help you understand yourself better. Along the way, I have learned so much from my challenges and losses in life and from the people who did wrong against me. So here are seven guiding points that can help you ride the wave of life. Just remember to take what you need, and if it does not relate to you, that's okay because my words will touch those who inspire to understand why life is the way it is for you!

Guiding points for life

1. **Let it go!**
   Never allow yourself to ruminate! Rumination is a deep or considered thought in life. Overly thinking and reducing anxious thoughts have an onerous impact on one's well-being. Do not allow someone else's negativity to bring you down. A bad day is just that! Do not let it impact the next day or the whole week. Talk about it, get it out of your system, whether it is through physical exertion such as taking up a new sporting hobby like mixed martial arts (MMA), having a drink, going shopping, or escaping overseas for a little bit of rest and recovery (R&R). Do it! But remember, you must acknowledge it is time to let the old ways have new ways come into your life. Hiding behind your tough exterior does not help you one bit. It just slows you down from truly becoming the best version of yourself! It is extremely easy to be fearful of yourself. I have learned to grasp my life by believing in myself more than ever as part of becoming unstoppable. No one has power over you, only you do. To own something, let the old stuff go, create new memories, and dream big!

2. **Ignore them!**
   There will be times you do stupid things, and you look at yourself and go why did I do that? Oh well, shit happens, and you just must keep bouncing along, in a straight direction that is not linear. What someone thinks of you is their business. I have had to learn to let things go and rewire my brain around this notion of people-pleasing. Who cares what someone thinks of me? This used to always play on my mind. I was always taught to care about others, to serve. Now it is time to rewire that pattern of behaviour. If people must gossip about you, remember it is them with the problem and do you want

to control the narrative? It just weighs you down and does not help you know what everyone thinks of you. Okay, we get a bit of external validation about ourselves from someone new. Of course, it builds upon the ego. But just watch out for these ego warriors. They may have other intentions that do not serve you as well. It is in these moments that again, rise above the mess and look above the mist. Making oneself a priority means doing new things, creating new habits, and formalising new patterns of behaviour. I have learned I do not need to know what others think of me, stop people pleasing, and believe in myself more.

3. **Take one day at a time. Time will heal you. Learn to have patience!**
When you experience a traumatic event, whether that is a breakup of a relationship, losing your job, experiencing the death of a loved one, going through an employment battle in court, or suffering a serious knee injury you must allow yourself some breathing space to walk through the mess. It feels like your life is in utter shambles, but I promise you, the struggle will not last forever. It is important to refocus, talk kindly to oneself, and have faith. People who hurt you are selfish and truly do not belong in your mob. They simply are not aligned with your values. Good people can make mistakes, but most times, people are ashamed of their actions and continue to run from their mistakes instead of facing all challenges head-on. I have experienced many hard challenges and have learned to be patient.

I started MMA fighting after a friend said I should come and give it a go. I loved the thrill and the chase of doing a fight. During the 20-week programme of being in ALTA and training at City Kickboxing I suffered a serious knee injury that meant for the last three months of the year, I have been learning to slow down. This includes learning to walk and allow the body time to heal. It is a huge challenge from going 100% of the time for my life to resting and being still in the moment. Striving to attain my goals, I set myself and simply just relaxing. I have learnt to listen to myself more, spend time more by myself and really analyse the actions of what people and others are telling me. There is nothing better than listening to silence and observing others. It is through the observation of other's actions you get to really learn about them. Accept silence and in turn, you will see if people are truly meant for you through their repetitive actions. Words are words, but actions and consistency are what you are looking for in people.

4. **Avoid comparing yourself with others.**
    Comparing your life with others is not serving your purpose. All comparison does it sets you up for failure and measuring oneself against others only affects your mental space and peace. At all costs, you must protect your peace of mind from those who bring drama to your life. At stages in your life, you must learn to be content and happy with where you are. From my point of view, comparison is where you are developing an appreciation of yourself, who you are, and where you measure up against someone. Comparing yourself with others draws on negativity and resentment, which has no place in anyone's life and can become toxic. The saying *kia tupato means* 'Be careful' that you do not '*takahi o te mana*' (stamp on people, friends), which means do not be nasty to others, be kind instead, or bad things will happen to you if you are the perpetrator of harm or unkind actions and thoughts.

The only person you compete with is yourself. Each day I get up I am becoming a better me. I have learned to let things go, particularly those things and people that do not serve me anymore or bring happiness, confidence, and peace. Each day I have worked on being a better person and that means doing the simple things well when things do not go well. Just remember, you can only control your emotions and reactions by shifting the language that you use to talk to yourself. One practical way to help you become a better person is to practice gratitude. When you are grateful, you acknowledge the things and people who serve you well. You focus on the strengths that you have as a person, and you work towards the areas that you consider are weaknesses. In the end, the weaknesses will turn into strengths, and this is more *mana*-enhancing than focusing on the negatives. Identifying what three key strengths you have will help you overcome your self-limiting beliefs and unravel belief assumptions you have. So, what are the three things you like about yourself?

The three things I like about myself are:

- I love to build strong relationships based on mutual respect, trust, and honesty. I believe in people and see the best in people. I enjoy helping others succeed and spending time with good friends and family. I love being with my people who get into being active, curious about learning, and trying new things that I have never done.
- I love that I am a learner. I enjoy growing myself and changing to become a better person. I love that I am curious, intelligent, and challenging of others. I enjoy talking and sharing my love for learning and for making the world a better place by starting with me.

- I love keeping myself active and involved in the outdoors. I enjoy spending my time at the gym and training for events that challenge me outside my comfort zone. Boxing, MMA, swimming, scuba diving and spending time in the outdoors at Mahia, Poor Knights and Cathedral Cove are my fun spaces that bring me peace.

5. Staying calm under pressure and in stressful situations
Managing stress and emotions is necessary if you want to achieve your full potential. To become the best version of yourself and experience transformation, you need some skills and strategies that will allow you to reach enhanced levels of success, happiness, and fulfilment from across all domains of well-being in your life. Stress can impact all areas of life if you allow it to. Stress is acknowledged by Dave Wood, the trainer and founder of Integrated Training, "as the body's physiological and psychological response to a stressor," (2023, p. 4). During 2023 I was placed under immense pressure and stress from a failed marriage, death in the family, leading and supporting *whānau* with a couple of Māori land applications in Māori Land court and learning to process change at a greater rate than ever at work. It was like all things were happening to me all at once. I felt I had no control, as the old Hazel would like to know everything. Well, that version has changed into something better from all the stressors I have faced. Sometimes it takes time to process, and you must take time out and reassess your new direction in life. On top of everything staying calm under pressure involves understanding the two divisions of the Autonomic Nervous System, the parasympathetic and sympathetic divisions. The adaption that the body makes over time from chronic stress and stressors in life can impede your happiness and self-confidence thus affecting your moods and state of mind.

I enrolled in Dave's workshop at Piha which I felt had a direct correlation to supporting me to become better at dealing with stress and learning to become more successful with overcoming mental blocks in one's mindset. I loved the outdoors and reconnecting with like-minded people who wanted to learn new skills and strategies to become better versions of themselves. Under intense supervision and within controlled environments, I learned how to manage my emotions better. I thrive in physical activity and swimming is an area I love. The designed activities had us learning to embrace stress, adapt our breathing to the situation, slow the mind down, and review and make shifts in the language we use to talk to ourselves. Being conscious of our breathing and recognising when the body is under stress by releasing the tension through reconnecting with nature. The three most challenging situations were sitting in an ice bath twice in windy and cold conditions, swimming in the ocean during winter, and undertaking pool work with a 10kg weight belt while scaling the bottom of a 25 metre swimming pool. These activities were very much like the activities that I did at Outward Bound. The only point of difference was Dave's workshop shows us how our body adapts and changes to stress from a scientific perspective.

6. **Keep smiling – build you up!**

As the saying goes, life is too short to be melancholy and waiting for things to happen to you. It is all about taking risks and doing the hard yards that nobody else is willing to do. One's happiness lies within oneself. Life just happens; it is what you do with it that matters. It would have been easy to wallow in a conundrum and hide away, but my sisters, brother, and my dad would not let me do that. I had to take the time to build myself. With my closest friends, I just did that and have met some wonderful new friends through MMA and with work. I am reminded to let my little light shine bright like a diamond. So that is what I have done, keep running forward into brick walls and leaving everyone behind me who serves no purpose in my future. If there is one thing I do well, striving and attaining new heights. I am not scared of failure because I have learned to regain my inner sense of being, knowing who I am and what makes me who I am. I am so grateful that I have had the many challenges in life to now see and lift my head above the storm that had happened in 2023. It is rather more common than you realise mean people are doing shitty things and thinking that they got away from it all. Hardly surprisingly, life has a bittersweet way of balancing law and order within itself.

7. **Go on holiday and invest in you!**
It is so important to take time out and go on holiday. After nine months of struggle, I came away with a refreshing start to 2024. I celebrated with a double New Year's in Auckland and Rarotonga. This time away in the Cook Islands was what I needed to reinvigorate and just have lots of new adventures. By refuelling and filling my cup of love for myself I came away with new aspirations to chase my passions for spending more time in the environment. I loved swimming and spent most of my time swimming in the beautiful lagoons in Rarotonga and Aitutaki. I fell in love with my time in Aitutaki. The swimming was so beautiful and with my sore knee I spent most of my time swimming to the bar from one side of the lagoon to the other side of the lagoon, instead of walking or cycling to places. I got my *tamoko*, purchased my first piece of art works from Shane, and participate in a new sport, scuba diving because I could not walk. Investing in yourself and giving yourself time to heal is one of the best ways to attract abundance and positive people into your life.

6 KEY TIPS FROM CHAPTER 13

1. Embrace vulnerability.
2. Be aware of the armoury you wear to avoid being hurt.
3. Appreciate you better. Start new daily habits and secure this for 7 days.
4. Let things go that do not serve you. Throw out the old clothes and better yet recycle them.
5. Dare to lead yourself to new places. Go traveling abroad but do the places you want to try. I loved Queensland and the warm weather.
6. Shame and fear are hallmarks of unethical behaviour. Do not let someone's bad treatment of you impede your purpose in life and being happy.

Take care of yourself, treat yourself well. The best years are still to come. Resetting and chasing my dream to travel is high on my priority list for 2024, including setting myself up in my business Auahatia – Innovate with Hazel and becoming a crayfish hunter by completing my Open Padi dive training course. I hope that by learning a little about my challenges that you can also face anything that is thrown at you. Just know that life is for living and sometimes you must just take a leap of faith and know that everything will work out for the best in your journey.

Afterword

As we come to the closing chapters of Hazel's journey, we find ourselves standing in awe of the intricate tapestry that is her life. Woven with vibrant threads of experiences, adventures, and the profound lessons that come with them, Hazel's narrative is a testament to the extraordinary resilience and strength that lies within the human spirit.

Hazel, a spirited and daring soul, has embarked on a remarkable odyssey, navigating the unpredictable terrain of life with grace and determination. Her heart, an expansive canvas painted with dreams and desires, beats in rhythm with the pulse of her passions. Through challenges that would have brought others to their knees, Hazel has emerged not only unbroken but strengthened, with a spirit unyielding to the storms that sought to dim her light.

Life, as we witness through Hazel's eyes, is a journey of peaks and valleys, a symphony of highs and lows that compose the melody of our existence. Her story reminds us that our perspective and responses to adversity hold the power to shape the trajectory of our lives. Hazel, with a wisdom beyond her years, has learned to dance with both the shadows and the sunlight, extracting lessons from every twist and turn.

The pages of this book unfold Hazel's evolution, a metamorphosis guided by commitment, perseverance, and an unwavering belief in oneself. Success, she understands, is not a destination but a continuous process, requiring the nurturing of seeds planted with dedication and watered with resilience. Hazel embraces the sweat and tears, recognizing them as essential elements in the sculpting of her character.

In Hazel's story, we witness the blossoming of a leader, a woman with a vision fuelled by hope and a profound dedication to serving others. Her commitment goes beyond personal triumphs; it extends to a mission of making a positive impact in the world. Hazel's journey is not solitary; it is a path she paves not just for herself but for the countless lives she encounters along the way. As we close this chapter of Hazel's life, let her journey resonate within you. May her tale inspire you to navigate your own tapestry with courage, to embrace challenges as stepping stones, and to recognize the beauty in every thread woven into the fabric of your existence. Hazel's story is a reminder that within each of us lies the power to shape our destinies, to weave a tapestry that is uniquely ours, and to leave an indelible mark on the world.

May your own journey be as rich, as vibrant, and as resilient as Hazel's.

About The Author

Hazel's path to self-discovery has been filled with obstacles that tested her resilience, from failed relationships to setbacks in her career. Each challenge she faced had a profound impact on her confidence and well-being. Whether it was workplace bullying or infidelity leading to emotional and psychological abuse, Hazel saw each hurdle as an opportunity to reflect, reset, and rejuvenate herself through the mechanism of empowerment.

This transformative journey led Hazel to a new chapter in her life, one that did not leave her emotionally wounded. By confronting her pain and accepting it as a part of her growth, she was able to reclaim her strength and redefine her purpose. Through inner peace and a renewed sense of life, she embarked on a path of self-discovery that shaped her into the person she was meant to be.

Hazel is a spirited and courageous individual with a heart full of dreams and aspirations. Despite the challenges she faced, she learned that her perspective and reactions to these obstacles could shape the outcomes in her life. As she navigates life's highs and lows, she gains valuable insights while pursuing her passions and discovering the true power of resilience and personal growth.

She understands that success is a gradual process that requires dedication, perseverance, and self-belief. Embracing the hard work and challenges ahead, she knows they are necessary steps in becoming the confident leader she aspires to be. Driven by hope, resilience, and a deep commitment to helping others, Hazel aims to make a positive impact in the world.

With each step she takes, Hazel seeks to inspire and empower not only her Māori community but also the lives of those she encounters on her journey.

Glossary

Ahikā	home fires
Aroha	having empathy, showing kindness
Atua Māori	Māori god (s)
Awa	river
Awhi	support
Haerenga	journey
Hapū	sub-tribe
Hauora	health and wellbeing
Iwi	Tribe
Ka mutu	finished
Karakia	prayer, Māori ritual
Kaumātua	elder (s)
Kia tupato	be careful
Kohanga Reo	Māori Early Childhood Centre
Kōrero	talk
Kuia	nannies

Mahi	work
Mahitahi	collaborative practices
Mana	Prestige, authority, control, power, influence, status, spiritual strength, and charisma
Marae	ancestral home
Mātauranga Māori	Māori knowledge
Mauri	life force
Pākehā	European
Papakainga	building complex
Patu ngākau	trauma and wrongdoing
Pono	Genuine, being honest
Pou	post, upright, support, pole
Pukenga	knowledge
Pūkōrero	speaking with authority
Rangatahi	youth, young children, teenagers
Rangatira	chief (s)
Raruraru	problem, dispute, conflict
Taha hinengaro	mental and emotional wellbeing
Taha tinana	physical wellbeing
Taha wairua	spiritual wellbeing
Taha whānau	social wellbeing
Taiao	environment
Takahi te mana	stamp on people, friends
Tamoko	Māori tatoo

Glossary

Tangata Tiriti	People who came after the Treaty of Waitangi
Tangata Whenua	The people of the land
Tangi	funeral
Taniwha	water spirit, monster
Taonga	treasure (s)
Te Ao Māori	Māori world
Teina	youngest sibling
Te Reo Māori	Māori language
Tika	being correct, doing the right thing, being genuine
Tikanga	processes and practices
Tikanga Māori	Māori cultural customs, cultural practices and protocols
Tino rangatiratanga	self-determination
Tipuna/Tupuna	Elder (s), ancestors
Tohunga	proficient expert (s)
Toitu te whānau hitori	honour family histories
Tuakana	eldest sibling
Turangawaewae	roots, place of belonging
Tūturu	authentic
Urupa	burial ground, cemetery
Wahine	woman, women
Wahine toa	strong Māori woman/strong Māori women
Waiata	song (s)
Wairua	soul, spirit of a person

Wānanga	discussion, talk and deliberating; place of learning
Whakataukī	proverb
Whakamanawa	uplifting, and empower
Whakapapa	genealogy and family connections
Whānau	family/families
Whānau rangatira	chief, leader
Whānau rongoa	Family as healing
Whanaungatanga	building relationships
Whangai	adoptee, Māori adoption into the family
Whenua	land

References

Arapere, B. (2002). *A history of the Waiohau blocks. A report commissioned by the Waitangi Tribunal.* https://forms.justice.govt.nz/search/Documents/WT/wt_DOC_112651044/Wai%20894%2C%20A026.pdf

Best, E. (1914). Tuhoe, the children of the mist: Ngā Maihi. *The Journal of the Polynesian Society, 23*(90), 84-102. http://www.jps.auckland.ac.nz/document//Volume_23_1914/Volume_23%2C_No._90/Tuhoe%2C_the_children_of_the_mist._III._contd.%2C_by_Elsdon_Best%2C_p_84-102/p1

Best, E. (1996). *Tuhoe, the children of the mist: A sketch of the origin, history, myths, and beliefs of the Tuhoe tribe of the Maori of New Zealand; with some account of other early tribes of the Bay of Plenty district.* Reed.

Binney, J. (2009). *Encircled lands: Te Urewera, 1820-1921.* Bridget Williams Books.

Damon, W., Menon, J., & Bronk, K. C. (2003). The development of purpose during adolescence. *Applied Developmental Science, 7*(3),119–128. https://doi.org/10.1207/S1532480XADS0703_2

Glen, A. H. (2006). Te Teko. *Historical Review, 54(1),* 30-32.

Grace, J. T. H. (1959). *Tuwharetoa: A history of the people.* Reed Publishing Ltd.

Mead, H., Ngaropo, P., Harvey, L., & Phillis, T. O. (2017). *Mataatua Wharenui - Te Whare i Hoki Mai. Huia Publishers.*

Moore, K. M. (1990). *Kawerau: Its history and background.* Kawerau District Council.

Ngāti Awa Claims Settlement Act 2005

Van der Wouden, A. (1980). The Te Teko Hotel. *Historical Review, 28(2),* 100-101.

Yukhymenko-Lescroart, M., & Sharma, G. (2023). The role of life purpose and passion for coaching in subjective well-being of sport coaches. *International Journal of Sport and Exercise Psychology,* 21:6, 969-991. https://doi.org/10.1080/1612197X.2022.2116469

Dr. Hazel Abraham

Hazel knows what it takes to create success and strive for her dreams. Hazel grew up in rural Wairoa and spent most of her early years in touch with nature and the environment. Hazel was raised with strong family values, of service, care, and humility. She understands the importance and value of having a strong determination to overcome challenges and persevere in life.

Dr. Hazel Abraham is a researcher specialising in the field of educational success for Māori, intergenerational cultural trauma, and STEM equity for Māori in higher education. Hazel's book 'Chase that Itch' is a call to action for all women who face life challenges and those who have shared similar experiences, young Māori who are dreaming of being the 'first in family' to attend and embark on a university journey, and for organisations who are prepared to challenge the status quo and create transformative change.

Hazel provides consultation to young Māori who dream of pursuing an educational pathway at university. She is available for mentoring support for inspirees who dream of becoming an educational leader. Dr Hazel Abraham is also available for consultancy on related research connected with mātauranga Māori and STEM equity for Māori in higher education.

As a sought after speaker Hazel shares her powerful story of resilience, grit, and determination. Hazel can share her 23 years of experience in teaching and leadership within mainstream schools in Aotearoa New Zealand. Dr Abraham brings to life her passions of leadership, and chasing dreams through curated empowerment talks on:

- ✓ The power of authentic leadership
- ✓ Learning to listen, learning to grow, and learning to serve
- ✓ Overcoming challenges
- ✓ The tools for empowerment and personal growth
- ✓ Staying on path, having a vision, and leading with purpose
- ✓ Indigenous ways of knowing and being
- ✓ Blueprint for succeeding as a first in family and Māori at University

Contact Hazel if you would like her to speak at your event

🌐 www.auahatia.com ✉ auahatia1@gmail.com

Appendix 1

The story of Te Teko

Te Teko is a sleepy little town nestled in between Kawerau and Whakatāne in the Eastern Bay of Plenty. For many *whānau*, Te Teko is 'the centre of the universe.' Te Teko is near the banks of the Rangitāiki river (Ngāti Awa Settlement Act 2005). Before the 1900s, Te Teko village consisted of McGarvey's hotel and store, the school, and the schoolhouse (Glen, 2006). McGarvey owned the land along the riverbank except for the school, from the Māori land of Hekerangi to Mokai and to about a half a kilometre west of what today is known as Edgecumbe and Tahuna Roads (Glen, 2006). During the early years, there were around eight to ten *marae* and a few settlers who had allotments on the swampy plains (Glen, 2006). McGarvey ran the store alongside the hotel, which provided hospitality and supplies for the settlers (Glen, 2006). At first the road from Rotorua to Whakatāne was rudimentary and was fully completed closer to the end of the nineteenth century (Glen, 2006).

Image 1. Te Teko, Whakatane County: The construction of Te Teko Bridge. Photograph taken circa, 1920. Alexander Turnball Library, Wellington, New Zealand. Ref: APG – 1045 – 1/2G. From *National Library of New Zealand* https://natlib.govt.nz/records/22534184

Several elements contributed to the establishment of Te Teko Village. First, the ballot of the land in the 1900s by the Government and the drainage of the land associated with the foothill run-off enabled more land to be used for production (Glen, 2006). Next, the Rotorua Coaching Company made Te Teko a staging point for their service from Rotorua to Whakatāne and subsequently, Thomas Seccombe's acquiring of land, which forced him to subdivide what was to be established as Te Teko Village (Glen, 2006).

In the early 1900s, the Government organised a ballot for land to the west of Te Teko. Thomas Seccombe's wife from Eden Grove Farm in Mount Eden (Auckland), applied and won the ballot for land by the junction of the Rotorua and Kawerau Roads. (Glen, 2006). Because of this ballot, Seccombe took up his land and his son, Thomas Thorne Seccombe took land closer to the east of his parents (Glen, 2006). These properties were swampy and very prone to flooding because of the vicinity of the run-off from the hills and small lakes in the foothills of Pūtauaki (Glen, 2006).

The McGarvey and Seccombe families were major landowners in Te Teko. On 1 September 1911, William McGarvey leased a section of his land for ten years and six months to the Rotorua Motor Coaching Company. The company established a corrugated iron sheathed quarters for staff, stable hands, housed coaches, and the horses (Glen, 2006). The Rangitāiki River was at this time only able to be crossed at Te Teko and Thornton by punts, and at most times, the coaches and motor vehicles required the horses to pull them up the riverbank (Glen, 2006). On 14 June 1914, William McGarvey leased three acres with a right to purchase clause to Ewen Campbell Sutherland. On 14 June that same year, Sutherland purchased the three acres which then became the sale yards (Glen, 2006).

Following the passing of William McGarvey on 17 September 1918, Thomas Seccombe bought the land north of Rotorua Road from the

McGarvey estate (Glen, 2006). In 1923, Thomas Seccombe was in a financial conundrum and initiated the survey of the village area by selling sections off to potential buyers (Glen, 2006). On 10 May 1923, a proclamation was made for Lot 12, DP 15785 to be turned into a public reserve. However, the building of a community hall did not eventuate until the 1980s (Glen, 2006).

The next step in the development of Te Teko was the establishment of the local shopping centre. On 16 May 1923, the first section of the land to be sold off by Seccombe was acquired by Wi Charlie Hunia (Glen, 2006). Charlie built a block of three shops on the site which included a bakery at the rear. A driveway gave access to the residence and the bakery on the rear lot (Glen, 2006). His daughter, Elizabeth married Patrick McManus who became the shopkeeper. During this developmental stage a picture theatre, billiard hall and a service station was situated in the central vicinity of State Highway 31 (Glen, 2006). In 1923, the government further subdivided this land into smaller farms, and the allotments were balloted out to returned soldiers (Glen, 2006). In 1925, Wi Charlie Hunia was transferred land between the sale yards and his shops. Lastly, between 1926 to 1927, other areas of land had been transferred onto various members of the Glen family (Glen, 2006).

The local hotel has been a central identity of Te Teko. According to Van der Wouden (1980), William Magnus McGarvey, a trader, established the hotel in 1870 and supplied provisions to the military forces in Te Teko. During those days, the supplies for the hotel were brought up the Rangitāiki river in a boat or punt. A whaleboat was used to ferry travellers across before the coach service was established between Whakatāne and Rotorua (Van der Wouden, 1980). Stables were added to the hotel, where the horses were rested for the next stage of the trip.

In 1891, Lord Onslow was on a tour of the district and stayed at the hotel. During his stay at the hotel there was a great party (Van der

Wouden, 1980). There have been various publicans of Te Teko Hotel. In 1911, Mr McGarvey retired and Peter Ganley became the publican until 1920. In 1921, Mary McGarvey took over and after that there were Robert Douglas, Earnest Louis Smith, and John Donald Shea. In 1928 Thomas Bower Dunderdale took over the hotel until his passing in 1939, after which his widow continued in the role until her death in 1961 (Ngāti Awa & Ngā Maihi Kaumātua, Tamaoho Waaka Vercoe, personal communication, 2018).

Rediscovering whānau, hapū and iwi mātauranga

An important part of my journey has involved learning who I am and my cultural connections. To do this, has involved searching extensively through several sources, including oral narratives from *kaumātua* and *whānau*; the *pūkōrero* (speaking with authority) provided by mandated speakers as acknowledged in the Ngāti Tūwharetoa Bay of Plenty Claims Settlement Act 2005; historical books from the Whakatāne, Rotorua and Kawerau district libraries; literature and evidence associated with the early traditions of the Urewera District (Binney, 2009); varying WAI reports connected to the *hapū* and *iwi* of Ngāti Awa and Ngāti Tūwharetoa; Native Land Court documentation; Te Rūnanga o Ngāti Awa research archives; websites connected to each *hapū* spoken on within Ngāti Awa and Ngāti Tūwharetoa and including reviewing the seminal work of Elsdon Best (Best, 1996), Binney (2009), Grace (1959), Moore (1991) and the narratives provided in the research work on the ancestors of Mataatua (Mead et al., 2017).

In accordance with Māori tradition and *tikanga*, I have checked the use of sources with the *ahikā* (home fires) for each *hapū* and sought guidance from *kaumātua*. The various works have also been re-examined by using the Native Land Court minute books. The validating of these sources is necessary part of being *pono*, *tika*, and respectful. For Ngā Maihi, I have sought the guidance of Koro Waaka and Koro Dennis, including having *kōrero* with the descendants of Penetito Haweā line (the descendants of Koro Eric Moses). The 19th century has been a major source in regaining my *whakapapa*. At the turn of the 19th century, Penetito Haweā was the chief of Ngā Maihi and was considered a feared representative of the *hapū*. Penetito was well known in the early Native Land Court. For Ngāti Umutahi I have sought the guidance of Koro Jimmy Rota, including having *kōrero* with the descendants of Rota Tarewa line (Rota was a younger brother of Koro Waikato Tarewa). The Māori land court and *kōrero* with Koro Jimmy have been major sources in regaining my *whakapapa* for this line.

As I navigated the doctoral journey process, the material selected is subject to interpretation and the people who may read this, including my *hapū*, need not feel this is the only version; but it is the one that, as the author has come to on the material and *kōrero* available to her. This section introduces the origins and formation of my primary *hapū* who have supported me on this PhD journey. However, the narratives recorded of Ngā Maihi may not necessarily be correct due to the changing nature of narrating historical events from oral to written form. On the evidence made available from the varying sources and in consultation with *kaumātua*, it is up to the reader to decide which version is most applicable.

Image 2. Ngā Maihi, Te Teko: The primary residence of Ngā Maihi at Tūteao Marae, near the banks of the Rangitāiki river. Personal collection.

The origins of Ngā Maihi

The principal *marae* for Ngā Maihi is Tūteao, which is located on the banks of Rangitāiki river (Ngāti Awa & Ngā Maihi Kaumātua, Tamaoho Waaka Vercoe, personal communication, 3.10.2018; Omataroa-Rangitāiki No 2 Trust, n.d.). Our mum, Te Whakaehe Ela Mei Waikato would always make the effort for her children to stay connected to our *marae*, Tūteao whilst we lived away in Wainuiomata (Wellington region) and in Wairoa (Hawkes Bay).

During several *hui* about *whakapapa*, *kaumātua* have explained Ngā Maihi were forced to leave the Waimana Valley. They were relocated to the Rangitāiki plains, near the Te Teko Golf course and next to the Puketapu *Urupā* (burial ground, cemetery) (Ngāti Awa & Ngā Maihi *kaumātua*, Tamaoho Waaka Vercoe, personal communication, 3.10.2018). According to *kaumātua*, Karatiana Dennis Vercoe, Ngā Maihi were already an established *iwi* within the Eastern Bay of Plenty (Ngā Maihi Kaumātua, Karatiana Dennis Vercoe, personal communication, 29.9.2018). It was not until many centuries later, that Ngā Maihi became known as a *hapū* of Ngāti Awa (Ngāti Awa & Ngā Maihi Kaumātua, Tamaoho Waaka Vercoe, personal communication, 3.10.2018). Best (1996) provides several interpretations of the origins of Ngā Maihi. The first version is that Ngā Maihi are descendants of Potiki I and hence, formed a sub-tribe of Ngā Potiki. Other descendants who connected to Ngā Maihi included: descendants of Te Rangimonoa, Tamaroki, Haerewhenua, Te Kahutupuni, Rangikawhaki. The descendants of Rangikawhaki come under the title of Ngā Maihi where it seems to be applied to his descendants from his second wife, Rangiwaikura. The name of Maihi was given by Rangimonoa, who named him after the carved facing boards of the gable of the house of Ruamano (Best, 1996).

Ngā Maihi of Tūhoeland from Ruamano

The second version given is that the name was derived by Maihi being a son of Ruamano (Best, 1996). This latter account is not clear due to the *whakapapa* starting with Tutarakauika. The uncertainty of this account is there is no evidence to say both were of human form. Tutarakauika was the name of the right whale and Ruamano was deemed to be a *taniwha* (water spirit, monster), who wearied of seafaring life and took up abode at Te Papuni Lake, east of Maungapohatu (Best, 1996). As the story unravels during the nineteenth century where Ruamano was living, the lake burst and then dried up. Ruamano travelled to the ocean to meet the new European arrivals but subsequently, his dead body was cast ashore at Nukutaurua. Apparently, one of Ruamano's large tooth was discovered at his former abode near Te Papuni. The Maihi account acknowledges when one of his children, Te Aomarama married Puhou brought her offspring into the genealogical line of Potiki (Best, 1996).

Ngā Maihi of Ngāti Awa

A third version provided by Best (1996) some centuries past, is that Ngā Maihi was also a sub-tribe of Ngāti Awa. Ngā Maihi were known to be settling the lands within Te Teko and alongside the Rangitāiki River. Best (1996) recalls statements made by Tikitu acknowledging that Ngā Maihi of Te Teko are descendants of Toi, Māhu and Toroa. They all lived mainly at Puketapu Pā, near Te Teko and also at other fortified villages on the Matahina Block (Best, 1996). This is very much aligned to the *kōrero* given by Koro Waaka about Ngā Maihi being banished from Tūhoe. It should be acknowledged that Te Kahu Hawea is the older brother of Penetito and is the line that I descend from. According to Best (1914, p. 86), the Ngā Maihi *whakapapa* is given below:

Whakapapa 1
Ngā Maihi

```
          ┌──────────────────────┴──────────────────────┐
    Rangi-monoa                              Mahi-iti = Te Ao-hurunga-te-ra
                                             Tu-te-ao
                                             Rongomai-a-rua
                                             Ua-wera
                                             Kai-nuku
                                             Nga-riri-taua
                                             Ao-marama
                                             Hao-ika
                                             Whata
                                             Tuhana
                                             Penetito
```

Ngāti Mahu of Te Teko

Ngāti Mahu of Te Teko were descendants of Mahū-tapo-a-nui who lived at Waikaremoana and who was of Te Tini-o-Toi descent (Best, 1996). After the death of Mahū-tapoanui's child, Hau-mapuhia, he left his homeland and resettled in Matahina. Mahiti was a child of Tama-urupa of the Tūhoean Ngā Maihi who married Te Ao-hurunga-te-ra of the Ngāti Māhu hapū of Te Teko district. Their son known as Tūteao settled on the Matahina lands (Best, 1996). During the reign of Tūteao, his people Te Marangaranga adopted the tribal name of Ngā Maihi after the former title was abandoned (Arapere, 2002). Tikitu also noted that the Ngāti Mahu division of Te Marangaranga lived at Puketapu Pā (Te Teko), Tawhero and Tawhitikaeaea forts at Pūtauaki.

In Figure 1 below depicts the ancestor, Tūteao. According to Ngāti Awa historians and researchers, the people of Ngā Maihi are descendants of Ruamano (Mead et al., 2017). The *pou* (post, upright, support, pole) sits within the walls at Maatatua Marae in Whakatāne.

Figure 1. Tūteao ancestor (Ngā Maihi / Matahina, Hekerangi). From "Mataatua Wharenui: Te Whare I Hoki Mai" by Mead, Ngaropo, Harvey & Phillis, 2017. Permission granted from Ngaropo.

The Tūteao: Poupou' tāhū (direct line of ancestry through the senior line, ridge post of a house) identifies the lineage that Tūteao (father of Maihi) descended from and his connection to the Mataatua canoe. The establishing of Ngā Maihi as a *hapū* is a result of the marriage between Tūteao and Te Whakarurumai-o-te-rangi who begat Maihi (Mead et al., 2017). According to Mead et al. (2017), the following genealogy for Ngā Maihi starts from Ruamano:

Ruamano
Maihinui
Maihiroa
Māhu-piki
Māhu-kake
Māhu puku
Māhu-tapo-a-nui
Te Rangitaupiri
Tāmaka
Wairere I
Te Aohurunga-o-te-rangi
Tamateawharepohe
Te Aohurunga-o-te ao
Te Aohurunga-o-te rā
Tūteao=Te Whakarurumai-o-te-rangi
Maihi (p. 211).

Ngā Maihi is an abbreviation of Ngā Maihi o Te Whare o Rumano (Mead et al., 2017, p.211). This house stood at Te Mahia, which was close to Wairoa and situated within the Hawkes Bay region. In the period of Tūteao leadership, the *hapū* were called Ngāti Mahu. The original name of Ngā Maihi was Ngāti Mahu or Te Whānau-a-Māhu; they descended from Te Mārangaranga of the Rangitāiki Valley (Mead et al., 2017, p.211).

Another interpretation of the origin of Ngā Maihi is acknowledged in 'A history of the Waiohau Blocks' (Arapere, 2002). It is noted in the History of the Waiohau Block report that Ngā Maihi had customary interests and traditions in the area surrounding Waiohau (Arapere, 2002). Best (as cited in Arapere, 2002) recorded:

that the earliest occupation of the area south of Te Houhi (in the present-day Galatea) was by a people called 'Te Marangaranga' (p. 14).

Best (as cited in Arapere, 2002) also recorded Tikitu, rangatira of Ngāti Awa as saying:

> the descendants of Haeana (Te Marangaranga), Tangiharuru and Wharepakau intermarried and in the time of Tūteao dropped the name Marangaranga and assumed the name of Ngā Maihi… Ngā Maihi are recorded as living at Te Teko among Ngāti Awa (p. 14).

The purpose of introducing the origins and formation of my primary *hapū* was to share the transmission of lost intergenerational knowledge to *whānau* of the future who may go on their own *haerenga* (journey) of discovery. However, the narratives recorded of Ngā Maihi from the various sources of *pukenga* (knowledge) may not necessarily be correct due to the changing nature of narrating historical events from oral to written form. On the evidence made available from the varying sources and in consultation with *kaumātua*, it is up to the reader to decide which version is most applicable.

Excerpts from my doctoral research of *kaumātua* narratives provide further evidence of oral knowledge on Ngā Maihi:

> Ngā Maihi our *hapū* originated at Tāwhana Marae above the Matahi, you know the Matahi-Waimana Valley Road, when you go up Matahi Valley in Waimana. Up that valley where the road ends, that becomes a track. It goes all the way to Maungapohatu walking track. Well, the first *marae* is Tāwhana, that's where Ngā Maihi. It's still called Ngā Maihi but we were a branch that got the boot. You know they used

to have petty arguments in those days and our branch of Ngā Maihi were told to move along and get out. They ended up in Te Teko. Now I keep reminding our Tūhoe tribe because they told half-truths to Te Pehi. TePehi went straight from there to Puketapu to see Tumatara Pio. Pio our scholar from Ngā Maihi, corrected all the stories and that's the information that ended up in the book 'Tūhoe' by Elsdon Best.

(Ngāti Awa/Tūwharetoa, Kaumātua 76 years old)

All the way up in the hill here, you can see it from here, from Mt Edgecumbe, Tarawera Valley, Matahina which is the old grounds of the ancestral people of Ngā Maihi. They were ancient.

(Ngāti Awa/Tūwharetoa, Kaumātua 84 years old)

Mum & Nanny Hazel

My time at school

Wairoa Primary School Award 1984

Wairoa Primary School Award 1987

Wairoa Primary School Award 1998

My time at school

Wairoa College Form 3

Wairoa College Netball Team

Chase That Itch

WAIROA COLLEGE
PRELIMINARY REPORT

Name: HAZEL ABRAHAM   Form: 3 PI

Subject	Mark % or Grade	Grade for Effort	Work Records	Comment
English		A	A	A top rate pupil. Up to date and working hard. KJ
Mathematics	A	A	A	Does excellent work at all times. CG
Social Studies		A	A-	A very hardworking student. She does things with pride and zeal.
Home Economics		A	A	Hazel's work in theory & practicals is a credit to her.
Keyboarding				Working very well and showing good skill development
Science	B+	A	A	Good grasp of the subject - lovely written &
Computer				Hands on experience

Attendance Record: — Good.   Homework — Good. Up to date.

Teacher's Comment:

Hazel is one of those exceptional and rare students that a teacher has the singular privilege of coming across in his career. Hazel is a top student in all respects: Intelligent, conscientious, courteous, keen and well-behaved. Well done Hazel, Keep it up.

Signature: Clement George Pinto.

Principal's Comment: —

An excellent start - well done!

Signature: A. McNair

Parent's Comment: —

Very Pleasing Report

Signature:

Parents are invited to discuss their children's progress in the College Hall at ..... pm on ....

Wairoa College Preliminary School Report 1991

My time at school

Wairoa College School Report June 1991

Wairoa College School Report Final 1991

Chase That Itch

PARTICIPATION CERTIFICATE

ELECTRICORP PRODUCTION SCIENCE FAIR

Hazel Abraham

This certificate is awarded in recognition of your achievement in exhibiting a science project at an Electricorp Production Science Fair

Dave Frow
General Manager
Electricorp Production

C. Bull
Chairperson
Organising Committee

28.7.92
Date

Administered by The New Zealand Science Fairs Board on behalf of The Royal Society of New Zealand in association with The New Zealand Science Teachers' Association and The Kiwanis District of New Zealand.

Otaki College Science Fair 1992

My time at school

Otaki College Entry into university

Chase That Itch

WAIOHAU WOMENS HOCKEY TEAM
2001

WINNERS:
3 Open Round Robin 11 aside
Sub Church 7 aside
Section 2 Winners

RUNNERS UP
Jack Mason 7 aside
Te Rahi Memorial 11 aside
Openning Day Tournament
Mataatua Te Arawa Hei

REPRESENTATIVES
B.O.P. Cotter Cup Team
Marewa Hale
Ashley Phillips

WAIARIKI MAORI TEAM
Sharon Clark

N.Z. MAORI WOMENS TEAM
Sharon Clark

BACK ROW: Ginny Latimer, Hikitia Ripaki, Sharon Clark (Player of the Year), Kelly Wilson, Ngamihi Moses, Renee Anderson (Most Dedicated Player), Hazel Abraham (Most Improved Player).
FRONT ROW: Hilda Clark (Manageress / Player), Jeanette Tukiri (Selector / Coach), Helen Tupe, Sam Clark Snr. (Umpire).
KNEELING: Marewa Hale
ABSENT: Tom Winera, Ashley Phillips, Awhina Bedford, Lisa Mc Lean, Jade Mansell.

 Te Kauwhata College - 2007
Staff

My time at school

NEW ZEALAND QUALIFICATIONS AUTHORITY
Mana Tohu Matauranga o Aotearoa

School Certificate

This is to certify that in the above examination in 1992

HAZEL AROHA ABRAHAM

has been awarded grades in the following subjects

SUBJECT	GRADE
MATHEMATICS	C

NEW ZEALAND QUALIFICATIONS AUTHORITY
Mana Tohu Matauranga o Aotearoa

School Certificate

This is to certify that in the above examination in 1993

HAZEL AROHA ABRAHAM

has been awarded grades in the following subjects

SUBJECT	GRADE
ACCOUNTING	C
ECONOMICS	C
ENGLISH	D
GEOGRAPHY	C
MATHEMATICS	B
SCIENCE	B

He mihi maioha tenei me ōku Waikato whānau
raua ko iwi e Ngā Maihi, ki a koutou katoa ka nui
oku aroha atu, e, me pehea atu he korero? Otira,

"E rere pepepe, e kitea anuhe"
(In the flight of the caterpillar, the butterfly will appear)

Anei ra aku kōrero na koutou i tuku mai ki au, he roimata,
he roimata, he roimata e kei aku kamo.

Notes

Chase That Itch

Notes

www.ingramcontent.com/pod-product-compliance
Lightning Source LLC
Chambersburg PA
CBHW041305110526
44590CB00028B/4254